Nikola's Passage

A two-part account of my stay in Bosnia
1999–2001

by

Graham Bavin

Pen Press

First published in Great Britain by Pen Press

All paper used in the printing of this book has been made from
wood grown in managed, sustainable forests.

ISBN13: 978-1-78003-056-2

Printed and bound in the UK
Pen Press is an imprint of
Indepenpress Publishing Limited
25 Eastern Place
Brighton
BN2 1GJ

A catalogue record of this book is available from
the British Library

Cover design by Jacqueline Abromeit

Sailors on a sinking ship knelt down and prayed to God
to save them.
And God spoke unto them and said
"Get yourselves into the lifeboats, then; I may be able to do
something."

Orthodox Parable

To Harriet,
Only read this after
you have heart
your lines TEEHEE;
Kendest regards
Graham

Dedication

With love to Lindsey
XXX

Stoja

And my thanks to
Mum and Den, Pete and all my friends in Brčko

This book is written from memory and I apologise in advance for
any errors.

INTRODUCTION

An overview of the Bosnian war 1991–1995

The countries that formed Yugoslavia prior to the war were Serbia, Slovenia, Croatia, Bosnia & Herzegovina, Montenegro, Kosovo and Macedonia. Throughout the land, three main religious groups came to be: the Slovenians and Croats practised the Catholic faith; Serbia, Montenegro and Macedonia were Orthodox, while Bosnia and Kosovo were a mix of Orthodox and Muslim.

Since November 1943, Josip Broz Tito had led Yugoslavia and maintained a tenuous coexistence between the differing ethnic groups. Prior to his death in 1980 he had given recognition to the Muslim communities of Bosnia, granting them equal status to the local Serbian community and permitting them to practise their faith unhindered.

Following Tito's death, nationalism swept through Yugoslavia as each state sought independence and chose to break away from the greater country, which was now led by Slobodan Milošević.

During the summer of 1991, Slovenia declared independence and so started a number of clashes between the Territorials of Slovenia and the Yugoslav People's Army. As a result of the Brioni Agreement, which recognised the independence of Slovenia, the Yugoslav army withdrew.

A month later, Croatia also declared independence and once again the fighting started, this time between the Serbs and the newly formed Croatian National Guard, who were also supported by the Muslims of Bosnia. The war was now about possession of land, and each side dug trenches to defend the territory that they had acquired. This was to be a long and protracted battle.

During the same year, at the end of November, the United Nations agreed to send in a peacekeeping force. By the end of February 1992, that force (UNPROFOR) had been deployed.

Slovenia and Croatia were now recognised by the European community. Bosnia, along with Montenegro, now saw the opportunity to gain independence and held a referendum. The people of Montenegro and the Bosnian Serbs chose to stay with the Yugoslav republic, but the Muslims of Bosnia, led by President Alija Izetbegović, wanted an independent state, and as a result the war spilled over into Bosnia. This had now become a three-sided war between Croatia, Bosnia and Serbia and was viewed by many as a religious war between the Muslim, Orthodox and Catholic faiths.

Initially, the Muslims of Bosnia and the Catholics of Croatia both fought against the Orthodox Serbs, but this alliance was soon to fail. The Vance-Owen peace plan, which intended to divide Bosnia into separate districts for the Muslims, Serbs and Croats, collapsed, and the UN failed to give the promised protection to those refugees that had gathered in the so-called 'safe havens' such as the town of Srebrenica.

Amid all the fighting, political leaders were jostling for the upper hand. The Serbian President Slobodan Milošević approached the Croatian leader Franjo Tudjman for a joint takeover of Bosnia, but Tudjman, fearing that his country would lose its newly-acquired European Union recognition, declined the offer, and so the war continued for another two years.

The heavy shelling of Sarajevo forced the UN to deploy NATO forces against the Serbs who occupied the surrounding mountains. As the Serb army withdrew, the Croat and Bosnian armies occupied the land, and in October of 1995 the warring parties agreed to a cease-fire; that November, a new peace agreement, the 'Dayton Accord', was reached.

To this day, the United Nations has continued to implement the numerous annexes to this agreement and, for the people of the former Yugoslavia, has maintained a very delicate peace.

CHAPTERS

PART ONE

CHAPTER 1

A PAINFUL MISHAP

My suit of armour felt jaded and dull; was it me or had the job lost its magic?

15 years as a policeman in a dull, commercially depressed town on the east coast of Norfolk did nothing to give one a sense of achievement, yet I used to love this job.

Just who was the know-it-all professor who wrote 'police officers should not work a 6–2, 2–10, 10–6 shift pattern; it is far healthier to work a 7–3, 3–11, 11–7'? What arrogance! I enjoyed going to the pub at 10.00pm with the rest of the shift; we could sit and talk out our problems, moan about the job and socialise as a family, but now everyone went to work and then, at the end of the shift, went straight home.

No longer did I feel part of a family; I was just a number, PC1025.

God, I felt so angry!

When the letter dropped through the door and said that I had been selected by the Foreign Office for a 12-month secondment to the United Nations International Police Task Force in Bosnia, I was ecstatic; at last, things were going right for once.

'Hi, Sheila! I must show you the photo that my daughter sent me; the length of her hair is amazing,' I said.

Sheila sat in the kitchen and chatted to my landlady, Jean. I liked Sheila; she was slim, attractive, mid-forties, with shoulder-length blonde hair. She also had the vitality and sense of humour of a 20-year-old. I guess that was what I found so attractive in her, or was it just plain lust?

In my haste to show her the photo, my foot caught in the strap of my kit bag and I fell over, causing the side of my face to collide with the door catch.

'Oh, God!' she said and I knew things were bad.

Jason, Jean's son, rushed me into the bathroom, and, as I looked into the mirror, my worst fears were confirmed. My face was a mess, with a cut that ran from my hairline past my left eye and down to my cheek.

'Damn, damn, damn!' I cursed. 'I must make the flight to Bosnia tomorrow; can you give me a lift to the hospital, Jason?'

'No problem,' he replied.

I pressed a cloth against my face and felt the warmth of my own life-giving blood oozing between my fingers and dripping onto my shirt.

Jason drove while I sat muttering to myself, 'I need this like a hole in the head,' then I chuckled at my own stupid words; I had got a hole in my head!

The night was cold and miserable as I climbed out of Jason's car; the howling wind caused the trees to make a *swishing* sound, but the hospital lights gave a soft, serene, welcoming glow to the entrance of the casualty department.

'So what have we done here, then?' asked the receptionist.

Oh, what a temptation; shall I say that I was bungee jumping from the bedroom window?

'I fell over.' Damn! You should have gone with the first option; why must you be so honest?

The doctor and nurses were very professional, and one hour later I was stitched up with 12 stitches above the eye and 16 below. I walked out of the hospital looking like Mary Shelley's Frankenstein's monster.

'Damn, I really don't need this!'

Sheila had already left by the time I returned to the house. Jean, however, had heard the car drawing up outside and had put on the kettle to make a coffee.

'Oh, my God, are you going to fly to Bosnia tomorrow like that?' she asked.

'Of course; it will take more than this to stop me!'

'Well, I guess I will have to take a photo for the album,' she said, and quickly shot off a few snaps with her camera.

I lit a cigarette, then took the mug of coffee to the bedroom and continued to pack my clothes for the trip of a lifetime.

'I hope this heals quickly' I said to myself.

I woke up early; the morning sunshine bathed my face with warmth as I looked out across the garden.

Two starlings fought aggressively on the lawn, each bobbing up and down like a marionette attached to lengths of string and both determined to retain dominance of the territory. Meanwhile, high above, a sparrowhawk hovered, waiting patiently for one of the birds to tire sufficiently before diving in for the kill.

'Well, there is a lesson in life for you, Graham: just when you think you have gained a victory, someone bigger comes along and spoils your day!' I mused to myself.

I sloped off to the bathroom, stopping momentarily to break wind. 'Phew! What did you eat yesterday?' I muttered.

Resting my hands on the sink, I leant forward and stared at myself in the mirror. The line of stitches formed an S shape around my left eye. In a strange way, I liked them; they gave my face character.

My mind now drifted off into a fantasy of explanations for how I had come by such a wound.

'You will never take me alive, copper; come near me and I will stab you with this!'

'She's gonna blow, but there is still a child in there; I must save her!'

'I will hold down the tiger; you run for your lives!'

Bing bong!

'Good morning, Mr Bavin; I am delivering your hire car. Can you sign here, please?'

'Yes, certainly.'

'That's a nasty-looking scar, sir; how did you come by that?'

'I fell over.' Damn, I said it again!

I threw the kit bag into the boot of the car. A glance at the watch told me it was 7am, and the village of Dersingham was still asleep. Spider's webs hung from the wing mirrors of parked cars and, being heavy with the morning dew, looked like carefully placed net curtains. The only notable sound that could be heard was the high-pitched 'clacking' from pheasants that roamed the woods on the nearby Sandringham royal estate.

'Time to go,' I said to myself, and I set off towards London Gatwick Airport.

As the flight to Bosnia was not going to leave until the following morning, I booked into the Gatwick hotel. The rest of the assembled team had done the same, and, in time-honoured tradition, we all met at the bar.

'Cum 'ed, Gavvers, which Judy gave you that?' asked Keith in his broad Liverpudlian accent.

'Well... oh, what's the use? I fell over.'

'I'm impressed; that really does look the bizzo. You will fit in perfectly in Bos,' he continued as he examined the stitches in detail.

Making light of the stitches did help to hide my own feelings of foolishness; in reality, I wished I had not fallen over in the first place. Besides which, they were starting to pull against the skin, and I found myself squinting to ease

4

the tension. Alcohol proved to be a good anaesthetic; the more I consumed, the less I noticed them, but after four pints of lager I just wanted to sleep (as Marlene Dietrich would say, 'I vant to be alone') and slid off upstairs to watch TV in my room.

I awoke in the morning to find the TV still on and flicked through the channels with the aid of the remote: news, news and more news, then a cartoon programme and back to more news. To hell with this; my throat was as dry as Mahatma Gandhi's flip-flop, and so I went downstairs to have breakfast and a cup of tea.

By the time I had walked across to the terminal, the departure lounge was like a beehive, loads of little worker bees scurrying around and then flying off into the sunshine to collect pollen or get a tan. Soldier bees stood guard at every walkway, armed with machine guns, to stop any unwanted foreign bees invading the hive and upsetting the status quo.

Beeep.

'Excuse me, sir, can you place your coins into the plastic tray and walk through again?'

I dutifully obeyed.

Beeep.

'For God's sake, I don't have anything metal on me,' I protested.

The security officer waved a metal detector over my body. I meanwhile looked at the man who was also being screened beside me and saw it was Richard Branson, head of the now famous Virgin Group.

'Good morning, Richard,' I said, surprised to be seeing him in the flesh.

'Good morning,' he politely replied and gave a warm smile as if we were old friends, before being ushered off to the VIP lounge.

'It was the buckle on your trouser belt, sir; you may proceed now,' said the security man, and with a gesture of the hand he waved me through.

The Balkan air jet looked all of its 30 years, and a visit to the toilet to get some tissue paper revealed black mould growing vigorously up the wall beside the toilet.

Once we were off the ground, the familiar *bing-bong* told me that it was OK to remove the seatbelt.

'You may smoke if you wish,' said the stewardess as she passed me my in-flight meal.

'Are you sure? What am I saying; you work here! OK, thank you.' Things are looking up, I thought.

The plane was only half-filled with passengers, so we could sit wherever we liked. Most people folded their seats flat to form a bed and slept. I, meanwhile, chose to view the world through the small oval window. Looking down onto the English Channel, I could see several ships criss-crossing the water's surface, their wake leaving a snail trail that glistened as the sun reflected against the movement of the water.

The plane continued to climb, and as we broke into clouds of billowing cotton my vision was obscured. I was left to my own thoughts. Pictures of my daughter Lindsey flicked through my mind, and I did indeed miss her.

Onward and upward we sped, into the vastness of the stratosphere. Above me was space; below, a new planet came to exist. Why didn't we land, so I could explore this strange, hypnotic landscape that changed its form every second?

My mind emptied, devoid of all thoughts as flickers of light skipped across my eyelids.

'Good afternoon, ladies and gentlemen; we are now landing at Sarajevo Airport. The temperature is 11 degrees and it is raining. Please ensure your seat is upright and all cigarettes are extinguished.'

My mind returned to reality, but the body was slower to respond as pins and needles darted up and down my right leg.

Snow-capped mountains that gave way to pine trees now entered into view; closer and closer they came, and then even closer, I began to feel anxious.

Suddenly the aircraft engines screamed to a higher pitch as the nose of the plane lifted towards the sun.

I fixed my gaze on the trees below. 'Oh shit, please don't crash into a mountain now,' I muttered.

I saw the crest of the mountain passing below me, and the plane started to descend again, as did my level of anxiety.

Berdump.

Back on terra firma at last!

The captain was right; it was raining. It caused my stitches to sting as each droplet of water crashed against the surface of my wound and reminded me that my face was scarred.

I hobbled my way down the steps from the aircraft, stamping my right foot on each step, willing the blood within my veins to circulate again. Halfway down I hesitated to view the mountains that surrounded the airport and wondered which snow-capped peak we had just brushed the dust off.

My brain registered a dull voice. 'Pardon?' I said, not knowing who spoke.

'I said, excuse me, I am getting wet!'

Well, that was just great: a duff leg and now the hearing had packed up.

'*Excuse me.*'

'Yes, OK, I heard you the first time!' Some people are just so impatient. Could he not see that I suffered from a rare condition called tangle-foot? I continued down the steps.

I had no idea where I was supposed to be going, so I simply I followed the line of bodies to a steel corrugated shed. As I did so, my mind registered a strange awareness. Where was the colour? This was like walking onto the set of a black-and-white movie: no colour, just different shades of grey on all the buildings, cars and scenery.

I waited along with the others to collect my kit bag and steel kit box; these we loaded onto a lorry which then conveyed them to our accommodation. I meanwhile climbed aboard a white UN bus and noted that not only was the leg responding normally again but so was the hearing!

The bus trundled along through the streets of Sarajevo. Staring out of the window, I could only catch glimpses of the large government buildings that displayed the Ottoman architecture. The town shouted its past; nothing appeared modern or new, that is if you discounted the many freshly painted mosques that stood tall like Saturn V rockets waiting to blast off to the moon.

The bus drew to a halt and everybody disembarked. I walked through the entrance of a wooden building that had been constructed to look like a German Bierkeller, but was in fact the restaurant and hotel reception area.

'*Dobro dan*,' mumbled the receptionist as he handed me the chalet key. 'You mist geeve me your passopot; I give back tomorrow.'

Bless him, I thought, at least he tries to speak English; how many of this lot speak Bosnian? Then I remembered that I did not speak a word of the local language and a pang of guilt hit me.

Back outside, I set off in search of the chalet that was to be my home for the next ten days.

'Hi, Gavvers; it looks like I am sharing with you,' said Dave.

'No problem, I just hope you don't snore or fart!' I replied.

Dave smiled and spoke again. 'This is where Torvill and Dean stayed during the ice skating championships back in the 80s, you know, when they scored a perfect ten and won the gold medal.'

'Really?' I mused.

I looked around at the small black wooden chalets. They were hardly large enough to fit a small car inside, let alone to be able to accommodate two blokes and all their kit.

'So where is the ice rink?' I asked, in an effort to make polite conversation.

'We passed it on the way here; it is just a derelict plot of land now.'

This was a shame, considering all the hard work that the competitors put in trying to turn an Olympic dream into a reality.

'D9: this is ours!'

Stepping into the single room confirmed how compact and bijou the chalet was. 'This isn't a chalet, it's a garden shed painted black!'

But my protests were unfounded, because, at the end of the day, it did have two beds, a shower and a toilet; furthermore, a TV hung precariously onto a wall bracket.

'Well, at least we can watch telly tonight,' I suggested.

Pangs of hunger now gnawed at my belly. There seemed no point in unpacking; I couldn't even if I wanted to, as there was nowhere to hang anything. A solitary bedside cabinet served as a tallboy, provided you were the size of an infant, that is!

I returned to the restaurant.

'*Dobro veče, izvolite,*' muttered the waiter, pen and notepad at the ready.

'Beer and spaghetti bolognese, please.' I must have a go at the local lingo, I thought; I feel so pathetic not being able to speak a second language.

I picked up the menu and studied the fine fare on offer. Coffee: *kafa* , milk: *miljeko*, cheese: *sir*, lamb: *janja*; hardly the most professional way to learn the local language, but I suppose it's a start.

The waiter returned.

'How do you say please and thank you in local?' I asked.

'*Molim i Hvala*,' he said, frowning, unsure as to why I bothered to ask, and then he placed the meal in front of me.

'*Hvala*,' I said.

The waiter just smiled.

Time passed quickly. I finished my meal and returned to the shed, or should I say chalet. Dave was lying on his bed watching the television; there was no sound or programme, just a red screen with the word 'EPOTIKA'.

'What do you think "*epotika*" means?' he asked.

'I don't know; maybe it means "epilogue".'

We both stared at the screen, blankly waiting in anticipation for the programme to start, and then it flickered into life.

Aaah, aaah, grunt, grunt, slap, grunt, du bist, ich liebe dich...

'BLOODY HELL!'

All 14" of the TV screen were filled with two naked, writhing bodies, going at it like two rutting wilde-beest, complete with the obligatory multiplex, widescreen, panoramic close-up shots, all in glossy colour.

Language lesson number two: '*epotika*' means 'erotica'!

I tried to will myself to sleep, but the brain refused to shut down. Across the room, Dave snored.

Snort, snort, fah fah fah fah, then silence.

Snort, snort, fah fah fah fah, then silence, continued silence.

I rolled over and looked across the room, checking for signs of life.

Cough, cough, snort, fah fah fah.

Post note to brain: *I'm going to kill him in the morning!*

I rolled back and assumed my original position, 'sleeping spoons' not being half so much fun when alone.

Dave stirred and threw back the covers; I could hear his feet padding across the tiled floor.

THUD.

'Shit!'

I lay still, quietly chuckling to myself: the only piece of furniture in the entire room and he had to walk into it. Thank you, God!

The tinkle of fluid occasionally interrupted by loud flatulent noises ensured that all my senses were fully alert. I sat up in bed. 'Are you OK?'

'Yeah, fine; I just stubbed my big toe, that's all.'

I lay back down and buried my face into the pillow to filter the noxious fumes that now emanated from the toilet.

Sleep came at last.

I had planned to indulge in a spot of breakfast, but time passed quicker than I could motivate myself.

Outside, the bus waited patiently for us all to board, then took us all to the UN military training camp in the centre of town. Walls of barbed wire surrounded the building, and as we passed through the entrance gate I caught my first sight of war damage; the cement rendering was peppered with bullet holes.

The bus came to a jerky halt, throwing everyone inside forward, the door hissing itself open.

In the lecture room, with desks and chairs set out like a school classroom, I sat and listened to a never-ending list of lectures. Here I learned the history behind the Bosnian war and the effects of ethnic cleansing. I also came to understand the current social and political state of the country and what part I was to play in helping the country return to peace and unified living.

The UN mandate for officers of the IPTF was described thus:

'*To implement annex 7 of the Dayton agreement by monitoring and training of the local police force. To ensure the freedom of movement throughout the country and to report any human rights violations committed against the citizens of Bosnia and Herzegovina.*'

Each day for the next ten days I was to return to the same classroom, and it was not long before my ears refused to listen to the endless droning of the lecturers, choosing instead to allow the brain to absorb the information via a process of osmosis.

The weekend proved to be more informative. Strolling through the streets of Sarajevo, I was in a better position to see the effects of the war. Some buildings were untouched, others bore scars, but in general the town carried on as though nothing had happened. All the shops were trading and sold top branded goods, the pavements bustled with shoppers, roads were filled with cars and trams clanked along tracks embedded in the road surface. Life went on as normal.

About a week had passed when the head of the training department approached me and told me to see the nurse in the Portakabin outside the main UN building.

The purpose of this visit was to have my stitches removed, but getting there meant driving along a straight length of dual carriageway affectionately known as 'Sniper Alley'. This long, open stretch of road earned its infamous title because of a monolith of a building, once the newspaper offices, from where snipers had a clear and unobstructed view along the entire length of the road. I was told that two snipers who had been shooting at SFOR personnel from within the building were promptly dealt with by the blowing up of the building with the snipers still inside, their bodies being entombed within the rubble to this day.

True enough, as I drove past the tall, black tower block I saw that one half of it was in a collapsed state, each floor laying on top of the other like a fallen deck of cards. The building now simply served as a monument to all newcomers that the town had suffered a terrible conflict.

The Swedish nurse was very gentle with me but wasted no time in having a dig at English surgery. 'Your doctors cannot count; you have 34 stitches, not 28, but at least they were tied well!'

The removal of the stitches was a major improvement; no longer did I look like Frankenstein's monster, and being told by the nurse that, due to the good stitching, my face would heal with minimal scarring was a great reassurance.

I returned to the chalet.

Of the 34 British officers in the team, only three were to be initially deployed to Brčko, a small town in the north-eastern part of Bosnia that, being only 150 kilometres from Belgrade, was a predominately Serbian area. This three-man team, consisting of Bob, Wayne and myself, stood waiting outside the hotel reception for the transport that was to take us to Brčko, then by chance a UN 4x4 pulled up alongside me.

'Hi, are you waiting to go to Brčko? Because I can take one of you with me, if you like,' called out Steve, the driver.

'Brilliant; I will let the others know I am going on ahead.'

I explained to Bob and Wayne that my getting a lift meant I would be able to arrange accommodation for all of us; this made sense and they agreed.

Having lifted my heavy kit box into the rear of the 4x4, I instinctively walked around to the passenger door.

'Are you going to drive us to Brčko?' Steve asked with a knowing grin.

'I don't think so; I don't have a clue where Brčko is,' I replied, and I plonked myself into the passenger seat only to see a steering wheel in front of me and only then get the joke. Feeling slightly embarrassed but happy to laugh at my own mistake, I got out and walked around to the other side. I just knew his thoughts: 'a new boy in town.'

The trip to Brčko was going to take about three hours, depending on the traffic, but I didn't mind; this 4x4 was very comfortable and did look smart in its white livery with large UN letters on both sides.

I didn't talk; instead, my attention was constantly drawn to the beauty of the countryside. Mountain valleys with heavily wooded slopes of deciduous trees were in the full flow of defoliating colour. Red, gold, orange and ochre: a complete artist's palette met the eye. And a broad but shallow river, the surface of which would reflect the sun and sparkle as the water gurgled its way over smooth rocks, cut through all of this.

Steve broke the silence. 'Looks peaceful, doesn't it?'

'Sorry, Steve, I didn't mean to be rude by not talking, but, yes, it certainly is a beautiful piece of scenery.'

'I know what you mean; it is hard to imagine that the Serbs used to execute people on the banks of this river during the war!'

His words made me sit up in the seat, as in my mind I pictured what would have been a most horrendous scene.

We continued north, leaving the river behind and heading up into the mountains.

'This would be a great place to go hill walking,' I said.

Steve pulled over to the side of the road and came to a stop. 'Don't get out, but have a look down the side of the car!' He leaned over and lowered my electric window.

Sticking my head out, I looked along the edge of the road. There, snaking along the kerbside, was a line of red tape, punctuated every 25 yards or so with a red triangle upon which was painted a skull and crossbones. Beneath this was the word 'MINA'.

'Yes, we are in the middle of a minefield, and where you are going there are loads of them, so be careful where you walk,' he said.

We continued on our journey and entered into the Republic of Srpska; this was indicated by the change from Latinate writing to Cyrillic on all of the signposts. It would be wrong to refer to this as a borderline; officially it was to be referred to as 'the Inter-Entity Boundary Line' or IEBL and defined the RS, which was predominately Serbian, on one side and the Federation of Bosnia, which was Muslim, on the other. But, if you were to ask any local person, they would refer to it as the border, despite the fact that both sides were contained within Bosnia!

The scenery now changed; the land was flat and open. Dotted about were a number of homesteads, all of which had plumes of white smoke spewing from their chimneys. A strong smell of burning wood filled the nostrils, and I could see pigs and chickens scurrying around the plain and unfinished houses.

We continued north and came across a large gathering of wooden huts: a market, perhaps? 'Have we arrived on market day?'

Steve laughed. 'Graham, welcome to the Arizona market. This is the largest black market site in the whole of Eastern Europe. Here you can buy anything, and I mean anything!'

We came to a crawl, so heavy was the traffic; it gave me an opportunity to view the scene of activity in greater detail. On both sides of the road small tables had been erected upon which, piled high, were packs of cigarettes, with just about every top brand that you could think of. Other tables were stacked with CDs, videos and music cassettes.

Steve pulled over by the entrance of a field which contained hundreds of cars, nearly all of which were of German origin, and, to my surprise, they were all for sale. I climbed out of the 4x4 and looked about to better absorb the mass of buildings and people that surrounded me. The wooden huts seemed to stretch as far as the eye could see. Some of the buildings looked more permanent in structure and proudly displayed neon signs with the word 'NOC CLUB'.

'This place even has a night club,' I quipped.

'Oh, yes, there are about forty of them on this site, but over here the words "*noc club*" mean "whorehouse",' Steve replied.

God, I thought, sex is a big business over here. I tried hard to keep an air of professionalism by not looking too intently to see how attractive the ladies of the night were.

A woman now stood beside me, clutching two 200-packs of a well-known brand of cigarettes.

'*Izvolite*?' she said.

I had already quickly learnt that '*izvolite*' meant 'what would you like?' 'How much?'

'*Molim*,' she replied, frowning.

'*Koliko kosta*?' interrupted Steve, coming to my assistance.

'*Dvadeset mark*,' she replied, demanding 20 marks.

'*Ne hvala, petnaest mark*,' Steve said, offering 15.

'*Sedamnaest, molim te!*' she continued, waving the cigarettes under Steve's nose.

All this bartering gave me the chance to study the woman in detail. She looked about 50 years old, slim, with long black wiry hair that was tied back with a headscarf. She wore a flower-printed dress that had been in fashion back in the 1960s and a pair of slippers that were made out of a carpet-type material.

Her weathered face shouted 'I have had a hard life', so I gave in and handed over a 20-mark note. She handed me the cigarettes and started to give me the change, but I stopped her and said, 'No problem.'

'*Hvala puno,*' and with a smile she left.

'This is some marketplace,' I said to Steve. 'Where does it all come from?'

Steve thought for a moment and flicked his cigarette onto the ground. 'Over here you have to apply a simple rule of thumb: if it is genuine it is stolen; if it is not stolen then it is a fake!'

I took out a pack of cigarettes, proud of that fact that I had foiled the British tax system by purchasing a top brand for a mere 25p sterling. Lighting the cigarette, I drew in the smoke deeply. Nicotine raced around the body's system and crashed into the brain, sending a mixture of confused signals and making me feel lightheaded.

I exhaled and looked at the writing that surrounded the filter tip.

'*Ronhill?* For Christ's sake, they didn't even spell it right!'

'See, you can have anything you like, but they are all fakes. Still, it's a smoke, and that's better than no smoke at all, if you get my meaning.'

I certainly did!

After climbing back into the vehicle, we continued north until we reached Lončari junction. Here we turned east and followed the Sava River to Brčko. 20 minutes later, we had arrived.

'Would you like me to show you a few places around the town?' Steve asked.

'Yes, I would like that. I am curious as to what happened here during the war.'

We passed the sign that told us we had entered Brčko District. Steve now turned off the main road and headed for the small village of Ulica. The single-width road was deeply rutted and full of holes that had been caused by mortar fire.

The rusting carcasses of small Yugoslav cars lay abandoned on the roadside; peppered with bullet holes, they now looked more like a kitchen colander.

The road opened as we entered the village, and my eyes opened wide as I viewed the total destruction that now surrounded me; not a single building was left undamaged. All that remained were the empty shells of houses that once contained life, family life, living and breathing. The sound of children laughing and playing, mothers performing domestic chores, fathers chopping wood or tending to livestock, all having a dream of the future. Only this dream had turned into a nightmare, as man's inhumanity to fellow man snuffed out the sparkle that glinted in one's eyes.

Listen! But there was nothing to listen to, only the ghostly whisper of the wind as it swirled in and out of the hollow houses. Or was it the souls of those who had perished, carrying on with life as if nothing had happened?

Where were the birds? Why could I not hear any birdsong?

Steve spoke. 'This is what is meant by ethnic cleansing. Every Muslim that lived here was either loaded onto trains and transported to Tuzla, 60 kilometres south, or they were shot and their bodies thrown down the water wells.'

'But I thought the UN were rebuilding homes like these.'

'In this area, you stay on the hard ground; the whole village, both land and buildings, is heavily littered with mines. You can't rebuild until the mines are cleared, and nobody is in much of a hurry to do that!'

The village was dead and had indeed become a very dangerous place.

Arriving at a crossroads, we turned left and followed the signs that led us to Brčko town centre, stopping outside a large corrugated metal building that backed onto the Sava River. This had been the abattoir. Here, Steve told me, was where the prisoners were held and killed, their bodies then being fed into the large mincing machines and the remains being pumped straight into the river.

'Oh, yes, I forgot to mention, don't ever drink the local water!' he added.

We moved on.

Stopping outside the railway station, Steve suggested that I get out and take a look for myself, so I did. I was not sure of what it was that I was supposed to be looking for, so I wandered about aimlessly, glancing around at the coming and going of people waiting to catch a bus. As trains no longer ran here, the area was now used as a bus station.

Nothing seemed untoward. Sure, it was a run-down building; so what? I looked across to Steve and shrugged my shoulders. He gestured for me to go to the side of the building.

What I now saw hit me with the subtlety of a sledgehammer.

The flat, white cement-rendered wall had a large circle of rendering missing at chest height; below this, bloodstains had blackened with age. Further along the wall, had wayward bullets left the now familiar pockmarks?

I examined the large circular area of missing rendering; here was the evidence I sought. Buried deep in the brickwork were the mangled brass heads of bullets, for this was a wall of death, a place of execution, and these small jagged pieces of metal served as a permanent reminder that human flesh offered no resistance to the spitting of an AK-47 machine gun.

Questions now filled my mind: why do people simply stand and accept their fate? Why don't they at least try to fight back? I could not answer these; never having been in such a situation, I could never be expected to, and those who could no longer spoke for themselves.

My heart grew heavy; so much sadness rotted in this town.

'The Serbs committed a lot of atrocities during the war, didn't they?' I asked, having returned to the vehicle.

'Yes, but don't go away with the idea that it was all one-sided; the Muslims and Croats both committed terrible crimes against the Serbian people during the war.'

It was true; during this war no one was without guilt.

Steve then told me that, during the height of the war, a group of Albanian mercenaries had entered the hospital at Bijeljina and had killed all the patients who were of Serbian ethnicity, then raped all of the nurses and held them hostage. Their freedom was gained only by the assistance of a Serbian gangster called Arkan and his army of mercenaries known only as 'the Tigers'. To the captives, Arkan was a hero, but to the rest of the world he was a murderous thug who rented out his services to the highest bidder and was accused of committing the worst of the atrocities. He was later to die at the hands of the Mafia, who assassinated him in a Belgrade hotel lobby.

I had seen enough for one day, so Steve drove me to the UN building on the edge of town; the blue sign read 'United Nations International Police Task Force Brčko'. This was to be my office for the next 12 months and I started to feel a little apprehensive about being here.

The building consisted of two white Portakabins, one stacked on top of the other; I walked up the staircase and entered a room where, against each wall, tables supported computers and keyboards. In the centre of the room sat a group of men and women, all in their twenties and chatting loudly in local language.

'Monitor Bavin, sir, I am welcoming you to Alpha Four and D shift; with us you are working,' announced a short Nepalese man, who introduced himself as 'Govinda'.

I took an instant liking to this man, who nodded his head from side to side as he spoke.

Govinda introduced me to the other monitors, a wide variety of people who came from such places as India, Pakistan, Greece, Holland, Germany, Spain and Italy, and then he led me to the group who were sitting in the middle of the room.

The group fell silent and stared at me intently.

'Does that hurt?' said a female voice beside me.

Startled, I turned to meet the speaker.

'Does that hurt?' she repeated, pointing to the scar on the side of my face, a scar that I had completely forgotten about and the cause of the intense stares from the others.

'No, not at all,' I replied, trying hard not to make my undressing eyes too obvious.

'My name is Beba; welcome to Brčko.' Her smile told me that my attempt to hide the undressing eyes had failed.

'Hello; my name is Graham, but most people call me Gavvers.'

'Gavvers,' she repeated. 'Well, in Serbian that is "Gavro", so we will call you Gavro.'

'Is Gavro a famous name?'

'Not really, but he did assassinate Archduke Ferdinand in Sarajevo and start the First World War!'

Beba sat down with the others; in ten seconds she had demonstrated that Balkan women were both beautiful and intelligent.

'It is time for *Dobro dan* patrol,' a voice said, and the room emptied.

'Trica, can you help Monitor Bavin find accommodation?' called Govinda.

'OK, then, let's go,' Trica chirped. She led me downstairs to another office, where she took three A4 sheets of property details from a folder and rang their respective landlords.

'This one is already taken but these two are OK, so shall we view them now?' she asked.

Govinda threw me a set of keys belonging to a tatty-looking pickup, and Trica and I set off towards town.

'So what is the meaning of "*Dobro dan* patrol"?'

'Well, as you can see, we have many monitors here, but none of them speak local; all they know is "*Dobro dan*", which means "good day". After that we must take over the conversation, so we call it "*Dobro dan* patrol".'

I decided there and then to learn the local language and do it quickly.

CHAPTER 2

WHAT A WASTE

Driving through the town, I could see people going about their daily routines. Many carried empty plastic bottles; these would be later filled with drinking water obtained from a gravity-fed waterspout in the middle of town. The tap was never turned off; the wasted water would merely be allowed to run down a drain, only to be sucked up and spat out again at a later juncture. This puzzled me; if the wasted water was allowed to drain back down to the water table, to be sucked up and offered again, then how did the water remain fresh and drinkable?

Watching the public also gave me an impression of the local fashion sense. It seemed to me that women under 30 would dress in fashionable clothes, small tops that exposed the stomach and tight-fitting hipster pants, all complemented with a pair of high-heeled shoes that exaggerated a woman's slim and curvaceous figure. And yet, by contrast, those over 55, who bodies had become fat and sexually undesirable, all wore black jackets and long black skirts. What was the cause of this strange phenomenon? Was there a particular day in one's life where the older woman said, 'That's it; I will wear black from now on'?

I pulled into the 'Street of Four Brothers'. Trica counted the house numbers out loud and gestured for me to stop about halfway along the street.

A woman in her twenties came bouncing down the tiled steps. 'Hellooo. *Ja sam Milka, dobro dosli do Brčko,*' she shouted excitedly.

Trica, translating, told me that the woman was called Milka and that she welcomed me to Brčko.

Milka explained that her mother would join us shortly, but in the meantime we were welcome to look around the house. Inside, I could see that it comprised a bathroom, two bedrooms, a kitchen and a living room, the last having a patio door that led out onto a veranda. The upper level of this large detached property was a copy of the ground floor, and, although furnished to a basic level, it had a welcome feel to it.

I liked it and told Milka, via Trica, that I would take the property.

From the hallway came a female voice. '*Alo, cao Milka?*'

'*Cao mama!*' replied Milka, as into the room walked a woman who I could only describe as breathtaking, looking like Sophia Loren's twin sister.

In perfect English, Milka introduced her mother, Stoja. I shook hands and looked deeply into her dark eyes.

Trica's voice jolted me back to reality. '400 marks a month is the rental; is that OK?

'Oh, that is fine.'

Stoja spoke in local to her daughter for a moment.

'My mother says the rent includes washing, cleaning and ironing.'

'Then I guess this will be my home from home,' I replied.

As I dragged my metal kit box into the hallway, the arrival of another UN vehicle signalled Trica and told her it was time for her to leave. '*Cao*, Gavro; see you in the Galaxy tonight.'

'OK, thank you for your help,' I said, then belatedly realised that I did not know what or where the Galaxy was!

Milka and Stoja helped me unpack; although Stoja spoke very little English, her daughter was more than willing to demonstrate her bilingual skills. Two hours later, Bob and Wayne arrived and the introductions were repeated.

'My mother invites you all to our home tomorrow evening for a barbecue.'

'That would be wonderful; please thank her,' I replied.

I awoke early; it was so quiet. Pulling on a pair of shorts, I stepped out onto the veranda. The sun shone brilliantly and, considering it was October, was so warm.

Basking in the morning sunshine, I surveyed the street. All the houses were basically the same, being large detached properties. Wooden panels and louvre shutters gave each house a sense of individuality.

I returned inside to make a cup of coffee, turning on the tap being something that I took for granted back in the UK. The water spat out under pressure and had a strange earthy smell. I decided against coffee and filled a glass instead. Holding the glass up to the sunshine, I saw that the water had a brown tinge to it and small filaments of fibre were spinning around in circles, and decided that this was definitely not drinkable.

The source of the water was a well that had been dug in the rear garden and was drawn via an electric pump fitted to the side of the house: crude, yes but very effective.

I could hear Bob and Wayne moving about upstairs, so I went up and joined them. 'Morning, gents; so what is first on the agenda?'

Bob wanted to go and check his duties for the week ahead. Wayne, meanwhile, was trying to phone his wife back in the UK, but it did not work.

'Try mine downstairs.'

He did, and a moment later he was talking to his nearest and dearest.

Breakfast consisted of a boiled egg and toast, after which we climbed into the minibus and headed off into town.

Tito had been the political leader of Yugoslavia since the war. Born and raised in Croatia, he spent his adult life in Belgrade, and although he died in 1980 he was to many a king.

Throughout history the Balkans had been a flash point for many a war-mongering tyrant: Alexander the Great, Genghis Khan and Adolf Hitler, to name but a few, and, in the main, the two most common causes for conflict were political greed and religion.

During the war, the Croatians had sided with the Germans, appeasement being an option preferable to having one's country blown apart. Tito in Belgrade chose the path of resistance, and with his army of Partisans, ably supported by the British government, he remained a thorn in the side of Hitler throughout the war.

For the Serbs of Yugoslavia, this help from the British was written into the history books and has been remembered ever since, which perhaps goes some way to explaining why I was made so welcome here.

In the town there were many tributes to Tito, monuments with soldiers raising flags and so on, but the most obscure of these tributes had to be the Ravena hotel. I am unsure as to what exactly the inspiration was, but here was a building, eight storeys high and built in the shape of a ship. What was the architect thinking of? There was no seagoing port in any direction for hundreds of miles, so where was the connection?

Opposite the Ravena was the blue neon sign of the Galaxy bar, and it was here that Bob, Wayne and I chose to sit and have a coffee.

A waitress quickly scurried over. *'Izvolite?'* she said. Stern and sullen was her attitude.

'*Cafa molim*,' I replied.

'Cola, please,' said Bob and Wayne.

She wrote down our order and, with an air of disdain, stomped off to fetch our drinks. Returning quickly, she slammed the two bottles of cola onto the table, making Bob and Wayne sit back in their seats. Then she placed my cup of coffee on the table and gently nudged it towards me.

I looked up, wondering what had caused the sudden change in her actions.

'*Prijatno,*' she said, before turning to serve another table.

Bob and Wayne looked at me with quizzical raised eyebrows.

'I don't know,' I said, pre-empting the obvious question.

I sat and watched as people came and went and quickly learned why the Galaxy was so popular. It was a long thin bar with sitting booths on either side, and the local girls would breeze in and look into each booth, then as if to announce their presence they would say, '*Cao cao.*' This was the perfect 'Paris fashion' catwalk, and didn't the guys just love it? This was indeed the place to be for any single, red-blooded male, and I promptly decided that this was to be my local pub.

Stoja's house was about half a kilometre away, along the main road, and as it was a warm evening I, along with Bob and Wayne, decided to walk.

Her house was about the same size as ours but was more established and looked more like a family home, with well-maintained gardens and a grapevine frantically wrapping itself around a pergola.

I pressed the doorbell and a pretty 17-year-old answered the door.

'Hello, you must be Grem; my mother has told me all about you. I am Rada.' She shook my hand as I introduced Bob and Wayne.

'You speak English very well, Rada,' I complimented.

27

'Of course. I speak German as well; we have had many monitors stay with us. Come, my mother and father are in the garden. *Mama*,' she called.

'*Molim?*' came the reply.

'*Ja imam Grem!*' continued Rada.

We all followed like sheep to the rear garden; it was mainly lawn, with shrubs growing in a half circle. A table stood to one side with places set for seven people.

Stoja wiped her hands on a towel and took my hand and led me to her husband, Dusan, who was busy cooking a variety of meats on the BBQ stove. We shook hands.

'*Dobro veče; ja sam Gavro,*' I said, having rehearsed earlier how to introduce myself.

'*Eh super, cao Gavro prica ti dobro Srpski*!' Dusan guffawed.

'My father says you speak good Srpski,' said Rada.

'Please thank him, but that is all I know; I have only just started to learn!' I replied.

'Good for you; people will respect you for that!'

Instantly, my mind returned to the Galaxy bar and the waitress.

The evening was pleasant and relaxed, going on until the early hours of the morning. Here we ate, drank and chatted about backgrounds. Stoja showed photos of other monitors who had stayed with them.

Dusan pointed to a row of bushes about 200 metres away and told me that during the war Bosnian snipers lay in hiding and shot at anyone who ventured out into the open. He then led me to his garage under the house and demonstrated how he and his family lived inside for two years, only coming out under the cover of darkness, and, as if to confirm his tale, he pointed to various bullet holes that peppered the surrounding houses. Stoja became a little short-tempered with him; it was obvious that she did not enjoy being reminded about the war.

Rada and Milka dutifully stayed on hand to act as interpreters for us all. I particularly liked Rada; being of similar age to my own daughter, her presence made me feel like a 'dad' again, and she did enjoy teaching me simple local phrases.

At the end of the evening, we chose to walk home, I am not sure if it was the excess of alcohol or the lack of street lights, but somehow we missed our street and spent half an hour trying to find our house.

The following morning I realised it was Sunday. The sun shone brightly, causing me to squint as I stepped out onto the veranda, but the warmth that radiated from the concrete floor was comfortable and inviting.

Bob and Wayne were both leaning over the veranda above me.

'So you are awake then; fancy a beer?' called Bob.

I went upstairs and joined them. Both were in uniform. 'Why are you in uniform?'

'We start our shift at 4.00pm; you start in the morning at eight,' said Bob, handing me a dumpy bottle of beer.

They left a while later, and, alone, I returned downstairs and switched on the TV. Middle-aged men and women were singing Serbian folk songs. The program was obviously dubbed, because the backing track would randomly speed up and slow down; this made for hilarious viewing even if I did not understand a single word. Bosnian television lacked the professional presentation that is often taken for granted by westerners, although, to assist in the improvement of this, the BBC sent a team to work with the local TV companies. Comedy seemed to travel well, as often I saw reruns of such programmes as *Only Fools and Horses* and *'Allo 'Allo!*

Boredom set in, so I picked up my Srpski phrase book and started to read, my peace being disturbed by the sound of the front door opening.

'*Alo, cao Grem,*' came the call.

'*Cao Stoja, dobro dan, kako si ti?*' I replied, reading directly from the phrase book but out of sight from Stoja.

'*Oh super, dobro sam, šta radiš, šta bilo novo Grem?*' she said as she walked into the hallway, knowing full well what I was up to and playing me at my own game.

Lost for a reply, I simply shrugged my shoulders. Stoja laughed, then, taking the phrase book from me, she quickly pointed out the translation for the words she had spoken: 'I am good, what is happening, what is new?'

We continued to chat this way for the next hour. During this time, Stoja loaded the washing machine and hung a new net curtain in my living room, then she left.

Dusk was approaching fast, and I did not fancy the idea of sitting alone in the house, so I put on a clean shirt and stepped outside. The walk into town was going to take me about 15 minutes. As I strolled along the pavement, cars and lorries threw up clouds of dust that covered the road surface.

Parked by the side of the road was a battered-looking car, and sat beside this on a wooden stool was a dishevelled-looking elderly man, covered from head to foot in dust. At his feet were several five-litre plastic containers containing what I assumed to be cooking oil but was in point of fact diesel fuel, which was being sold on the black market.

I continued on my way.

Passing under the old railway bridge that spanned the road, I could see the old 'Zetor' tractor factory, and, although it was closed down, security guards still manned the site, presumably ready to start up again when the economic infrastructure was more stable.

In the distance I could see the blue neon lights of the Galaxy bar beckoning me to enter, so I did. Loud pop music was playing.

'*Izvolite?*' asked the woman standing behind the bar.

'*Pivo molim*,' I replied, pointing to the array of bottled beers on the shelf.

The waitress then babbled on so fast that I could not understand a single word. I hesitated and looked blank.

'She asked you if local beer was OK, Gavro,' said a man standing beside me.

'Yes, local beer is fine. How do you know my name?'

The man laughed. 'Everyone is talking about the new scar-faced monitor from England who is trying to talk local. My name is Dragan, by the way.'

We shook hands and he passed me a bottle of 'Nik' beer, then he gestured for me to sit in one of the booths.

'You speak English very well.'

'It was the only subject at school that I enjoyed; now I am a language assistant on D shift.' He then tapped my bottle with his and said, '*Zivili.*'

'*Zivili,*' I repeated.

'Wait!' he said. 'When you say "*zivili*" you must look into the eyes of the person you toast, or it is a sign of dishonesty.'

We repeated the toast and looked into each other's eyes, exaggerating the action then laughing out loud.

I quickly relaxed in Dragan's company; conversation came easy and it was not long before more beers were ordered.

'I must say, I do like the name Dragan,' I said.

'Why?' he replied, deeply furrowed lines creasing his forehead as he frowned.

'It is a macho name: Dragon, a fire-breathing monster that ate knights in shining armour who were trying to save damsels in distress!'

Dragan laughed loudly. 'Do you mean like St George and the slaying of the dragon?'

'Yes, that's it; the English flag is based on the cross of St George!'

'Mate, I think you need to go to church and understand the true meaning behind St George, and as for the name "Dragan", well, when translated into English it means "sweetheart", so there is nothing "macho" about that!'

Feeling just a little embarrassed at my own ignorance, I apologised, but I need not have worried as Dragan found the whole conversation amusing and not offensive.

He left me sitting alone, but returned quickly and handed me a small notebook. 'Now, when you hear a phrase in local, write down how that phrase sounds to you. I will then write down the correct way to write it and give you the translation; this way you will learn our language very quickly,' he said.

And so, armed with pen and notepad, I spent the evening writing down phrases that I had overheard people saying. As the night wore on, total strangers were approaching me, asking if they could add to my list of phrases, and by the end of the evening I had made a lot of new local friends.

Dragan and I finished our drinks and stepped outside. The late night air filled my lungs and was such a pleasant contrast to the dense tobacco smoke that filled the bar.

'Where is your UN truck?' asked Dragan.

'I do not have one yet; I walked into town this evening.'

'OK, then I will give you a lift home,' he said.

I awoke well before the alarm went off. Having showered and dressed, I was picked up by a UN truck and taken to the IPTF station to start my first day of work.

When I walked into the Portakabin, Govinda rushed up to me. 'Good morning, Monitor Bavin, sir; today you are working with the Intervention group; your language assistant is Dragan,' he said, smiling and bowing repeatedly with his hands in the prayer position.

'Good morning and thank you, Govinda. Do you have a vehicle for me?'

'Yes, sir, I am having a very nice four-runner for you, but, I am sorry, it is not being shiny cleaning,' he said, with an apologetic head-nodding from side to side.

I returned downstairs. Dragan was standing beside the vehicle.

'Morning, mate; if you are ready, we can go,' he said.

We climbed aboard, and I swiped my driver card in the car-log. This small credit-card-sized piece of plastic was the UN's way of recording who was using the vehicle; it was also needed to allow the vehicle to start.

As I drove past the fuel depot, I saw Beba standing beside another UN vehicle. She smiled and waved, so I waved back.

'So you have met Beba, then?' asked Dragan.

'Yes, on the day I arrived in Brčko.'

'She is dating Velibor, but it will not last. Do you like her?'

'Let me put it this way, Dragan: she is far more attractive than you are!'

He smiled but made no further comment.

Having driven through the town, we arrived at the local police station and walked into the duty officer's office. I knew what the UN expected of me, but Dragan felt the need to explain the job in hand. 'We sit in the office until the intervention group get deployed, then we go with them and you report what happens.'

Well, that sounded straightforward enough, I thought, and I promptly sat down on a storage heater.

The office, like the rest of the building, was a typical eastern block construction: old, run down and in dire need of refurbishment. Cream gloss paint on the walls had faded with age and large portions of it peeled away like the petals of a flower. A single clear light bulb illuminated the room and hung like an overripe pear from a heavy-duty cable that protruded from the ceiling; nobody bothered with such devices as lampshades.

At a small wooden table two local police officers sat facing each other. Elija was the duty officer; he was cold and abrupt, but this was due to the fact that he did not speak English. The other was called Niko, and, although his English was limited, he was warm and friendly and welcomed me to Brčko.

A short while later, everybody started to leave the room.

'Let's go, mate; it is time for briefing' said Dragan.

I followed without question.

We walked upstairs and entered a large room; there I could see about 30 local officers sitting at rows of tables, and the room was full of chatter.

After a few minutes, the room fell silent as everyone stood up and in walked the chief of uniformed police, Pero Duric.

'*Sjesti*!' he barked, and everyone sat down.

Pero was a short, stocky man in his fifties; his weathered face showed age, but he did have great presence. As he spoke, he held a cigarette between his thumb and forefinger with an upturned hand, and this, coupled with a deep, aggressive voice, fitted my impression of a Russian general. Dragan translated his words; in short, he was telling off his officers about their untidy uniforms and some being late for duty.

At the conclusion of the briefing, Dragan and I walked along the corridor to Pero's office, to be formally introduced. The office door was heavily padded in black button down leather, so one was forced to knock on the doorframe.

'*Da*,' came the reply.

Dragan entered the room first and dealt with the introductions. Pero, now understanding that I came from England, had a complete change of attitude and welcomed me. He gestured for me to sit in the low leather chair and shouted to his secretary to bring coffee for us all.

This was to be an education in Serbian business etiquette. Put simply: if you have something important to discuss, you do not mention it straight away. First you must have coffee and a cigarette and then talk about the weather or the family.

'Pero asks do you have a wife back in England?' said Dragan, translating.

'No, I am divorced,' I replied.

'*Ne problem, Brčko ima puno naljepša zena, jedna samo za tebe, sigurno!*' boasted Pero.

Dragan laughed. 'He said that Brčko has lots of beautiful women; there is one for you for sure!'

I complimented Pero on his method of promoting East–West relations and thanked him for the coffee. Dragan and I then returned to the office downstairs, and before long the shift was over.

The next day, I was on night duty.

The Intervention group was a band of eight local police officers; their job was to attend any incident that may hold a degree of personal danger. This could range from arresting a suspect to subduing a riot.

As before, I attended the shift briefing, but now I had to go immediately with the intervention group to a café bar on the edge of town.

I, along with Dragan and the group of local police, entered the bar. The single-storey building had blacked-out windows, and as the front door opened the stench of stale beer, heavily mingled with tobacco smoke, wafted out into the street.

Inside stood a woman, the barmaid, dressed in teenager-style short skirt and tight-fitting low-cut top. Her breasts no longer had their own youthful support and burst out of the top like two exploding cushions. She stood leaning over the bar and smoking a cigarette, her back arched as if ready to be taken from behind.

'*Dobro veče, šta radiš?*' Niko asked.

The woman explained that someone had tried to force their way into the bar after she had closed and locked the door. She drew deeply on her cigarette and blew out the smoke, which hung in the air like a ghostly apparition.

Niko reassured her and said that one of his officers would escort her home. At this, she relaxed and offered the officers a drink.

Being my first night duty, the local police were unsure as to how I would react to such an offer and asked if I would like to have a drink.

I looked around at the group. 'Yes, I will have a coffee, thank you.'

Eyes fell to the floor in disappointment.

'And maybe a small Rakija?' I added.

'OOPAH!' they all cried, as each officer collected a small measure of the fiery spirit and sat down beside me.

'Do not worry; you will be safe with us,' said Niko.

His words were soon to be put to the test, as moments later we were called to attend another café bar on the other side of town. As we approached, the local police in the car ahead stopped an oncoming vehicle containing four men. I pulled up behind the police car, and Dragan took hold of my arm.

'Stay in the car, mate; those are Belgrade plates, Russian Mafia. We may have trouble here!' he said in a serious voice.

The police surrounded the car with guns drawn and pointed at the occupants. Slowly and deliberately, the men got out with hands raised, and each in turn was searched.

From one man, two hand grenades were removed from his jacket pockets, from another, a Russian pistol, and from the boot of the car an AK-47 assault rifle.

I could feel my heart pounding in my chest; my gaze was fixed on the activity around me, but mentally I was thinking of escape routes should matters get messy.

The weapons were seized, and the vehicle and its occupants were escorted to the border half a mile down the road, then sent on their way.

But this was not the incident that we were sent to deal with, so now we continued to the café bar.

The bar was in fact an ordinary house, the ground floor of which had been converted into an unlicensed drinking den and frequented by hardliners from the criminal underworld. The room was dark, and being lit by a solitary candle that cast our shadows on the bare brick walls made the place that much more sinister.

My eyes darted back and forth, looking for any signs of sudden movement, but the presence of the local police ensured that everybody remained still.

Four men, all in their fifties, sat at the only wooden table in the room. Another man stood beside a pool table, tucking in his shirt; his hands shook as he did up the fly buttons of his trousers, and sat on the edge of the pool table was a skinny 14-year-old girl with long, dark, matted hair.

The girl was taken outside by one of the officers, while the others checked the identity papers of the men and searched each in turn.

The bar was shut down, never to reopen again.

Dragan and I followed the police as the girl was taken back to her home in the Muslim quarter of town. On reaching a derelict house, the police stopped and banged on the door of the property.

A seedy-looking man answered. He was asked to confirm that the girl was his daughter. The man replied, 'No,' but he allowed the girl to stay at his house as though she were his daughter.

At this the girl laughed. 'Only because you want me to sleep with you for nothing!'

She then started to shout abuse at the local police, blaming them for taking away her only source of income.

We could do no more and left.

Niko climbed into the back of my 4x4. He enjoyed the opportunity to sit in a UN vehicle as we drove back to the local police station.

'So, Niko, have you always lived in Brčko?'

'No, I come from a village called Vitanovici Gornji, outside the district.'

'Would you not like to return one day?'

'Oh, yes, when my home is rebuilt I will be happy to return. In my village, before the war, Serbs and Croats lived together as friends, and then the Serbian army came and blew up all of our homes,' he said, with an air of sadness in his voice.

It had been a savage and brutal war, and sometimes life forced people into situations that they did not want to be part of.

As we walked up the steps of the local police station, we entered into a large open hallway. Over by the staircase was a wooden bench, and sat upon this was a scruffy-looking man who was obviously drunk. He stared at me hard through drunken eyes and shouted obscenities in local language.

Elija walked over to the man and shouted at him, but this only caused the man to shout more abuse.

A police officer was not a man to be disobeyed, and Elija slapped the man across the face, then spoke quietly but firmly to him through gritted teeth.

The drunk sat bolt upright, as if given an electric shock, and did not utter another word. He was then left to sit alone.

'Is anyone guarding him?' I asked Niko.

'Who, him? No, he will sit there till morning and be allowed to go when he is sober.'

'So what is to stop him from getting up and walking off now?'

Niko looked at Dragan and smiled. 'We shoot him!' he said.

I was not sure if he was being serious or just joking, but it did seem to be a logical answer.

'I am hungry; let us eat at the bakery,' suggested Dragan.

Dragan, Niko and I walked the 50 metres to the bakery, which was the only place in town that sold hot food and drinks at two in the morning. We sat at a table and a waitress quickly joined us, holding a notepad.

'*Izvolite*?' she asked.

Dragan spoke first. '*Pica sa ljuti ketcup, jogat i cola molim.*' Though he spoke local, even I could understand that order!

She then faced Niko.

'*Meso burek i jogat i cola molim,*' he said.

The waitress now turned towards me. I was determined to practice my local language skills at every opportunity and, knowing that the word 'isto' meant 'the same as', proudly said, '*Isto molim.*'

The waitress stopped writing and looked me sternly in the eye. '*Sta isto?*' she barked, waving both hands at me.

Dragan and Niko crossed their legs and turned away from me, both desperately trying to stifle howls of laughter. I could feel myself starting to blush; I was not prepared for this response.

'*Sta isto!*' she repeated sternly. '*Isto pica?*' she said, pointing to Dragan. '*Isto burek?*' she continued, pointing to Niko.

I now realised my mistake and looked towards Dragan for help, but his stifled laughter and bouncing shoulders told me that I was on my own.

'*Isto burek molim,*' I said meekly.

I was at this woman's mercy; she knew this and was not going to let me off so easy. '*Dobro, meso ili sir burek?*' she asked.

Dragan now howled with laughter, and tears ran down his cheeks. 'She said meat or cheese burek?' he spluttered.

My confidence returned and I politely said, '*Meso burek molim.*'

'*Dobro*,' she replied, and with a wry grin she walked away.

The waitress returned promptly, with our entire order balanced on one arm. She served each of us, leaving me until last, then, running her fingers through my hair, she said, '*Prijatno*,' before leaving to serve another table.

'Oopah! I think she likes you,' said Niko.

'Sod off!' I replied, and I started to eat my meal, but not before thinking 'that will teach you to be clever' to myself.

Niko and Dragan chatted in local; I sat in silence and viewed the surrounding activity. Occasionally, I would catch the waitress looking at me, smiling, then she would turn away to serve another customer. Did she like me? I wondered.

Dragan then told a joke about a woman giving oral sex to a man, the punchline of which resulted in white yoghurt being sprayed over the trousers of Niko and myself. It was crude but very funny, and this was our cue to leave.

We returned to the police station, and, after I had written my reports, the shift finished.

The next two nights passed quietly. I had not seen Dragan, as he had been off duty. During his absence I had worked with other language assistants and had got on well with them; each had their own experience of life during the war years and was happy to discuss this with me. Niko was now on day shift, as our duties did not always coincide.

Tonight was the last of my night duties, then I would have four days off. As usual, I was sitting on the storage heater when Dragan walked into the office.

'*Cao, dobro veče,*' he said to everyone in the room, and they responded likewise. Then he turned to me and, punching me on the arm, said, 'Hello, mate!'

He walked over to the television and tried to improve the picture. When the picture failed to improve, he banged the palm of his hand against the side of the set; this made the TV go off completely! A crescendo of voices filled the room in protest, so Dragan banged the TV again and the picture returned; he just shrugged his shoulders and smiled, followed by a lot of high-five hand slapping.

Suddenly the telephone rang. The duty officer answered and then shouted across the hallway. Opposite, a door burst open and out spilled a rush of police officers, putting on hats and strapping pistols around their waist.

'Let's go, mate, hurry, don't lose them!' said Dragan.

We ran to our 4x4, while eight burly police officers crammed themselves into two battered old police cars. I was surprised by how fast a ten-year-old Yugoslav car accelerated and had a job to keep up as they dodged their way through the town. My heart started pounding and I was getting anxious, wondering what incident had caused this response.

The officers pulled up outside a motel and ran inside. Dragan and I followed.

In a room on the first floor, slumped over a sofa, was a young woman in her twenties. She was dressed and looked attractive, but her body was lifeless.

The smell of death filled the room; I knew this smell well, as I had experienced it before as a policeman in Norfolk. A butcher's-shop smell was the only way to describe it, but this time it was mingled with the sweet odour of perfume from the woman's body.

A pistol on the floor and a single shot to the head told the sad story.

Why? I wondered. What could have happened to make her take such extreme and final measures?

41

The answer was soon explained. For over a year, the girl, who was a Muslim, had been secretly dating a young man who was a Serb. Then the inevitable occurred: the girl fell pregnant and chose to tell her parents before telling her boyfriend. Her parents were angry and told her to leave the house; thinking that a life with her lover would be better than a life of anger from her family, she obeyed and went to meet him. The young man, however, had also been under pressure to end the relationship, and now the thought of an impending birth was too much to cope with, so he left. She was now alone, pregnant and with no one to turn to.

Nobody knew how the girl had obtained the pistol, but tonight, as if in a scene from a Shakespeare play, she had ended her existence.

'What a total waste of life,' I said.

'This is Bosnia,' replied Dragan.

Outside was a hive of activity. The incident was handed over to the crime police, and we returned to the local police station. As we walked up the steps, more officers came spilling out.

'Looks like we are off again!' said Dragan, and indeed we were, this time heading for another part of town.

We arrived at the scene quickly; officers were kneeling on the ground beside a teenage boy, who was crying out in obvious pain.

'We need light!' shouted one of the officers.

I shone my torch onto the boy's arm; it was severed just below the elbow, with the forearm and hand completely missing.

We worked hard and fast to stem the bleeding.

'*Zašto? Zašto?*' cried the boy's mother; I knew what she was saying: 'why?'

Dragan comforted the woman, and his maturity and compassion impressed me.

Later he returned and told me what had happened. It appeared that the boy had gone to a party with his girlfriend, but at the end of the party the girl had gone off with someone else. Feeling hurt, he took a grenade from his father's cupboard and pulled the pin, holding onto the grenade until it exploded.

'It is a miracle that he is still alive,' I said.

'It was a blast grenade; the other type would have killed him for sure,' replied Dragan.

'What is the matter with the people of this town? Is life so worthless?' I asked.

'Mate, Christmas is coming and so this will be the silly season; we will get a lot of this from now on,' he explained.

We carefully lifted the boy into the police car and he was driven to the hospital. He survived his ordeal, but I felt he would long regret this night.

CHAPTER 3

CHRISTMAS AND NEW YEAR 2000

Two months had passed quickly; too quickly for my liking, but I did not have the power to slow down time itself. However, during these two short months I had learned some very valuable life lessons. Of these, the most profound were:

> *Not all sharks eat flesh,*
> *Not all birds can fly,*
> *Not all Muslims were fanatical and*
> *Not all Serbs were murdering thugs.*

Having accepted the facts of the first pair of lessons, I was honoured to receive the second.

Phyloxenia. The receiving and welcoming of a stranger into your home. The washing of his hands and feet, the giving of food and drink, and the offering of a place to rest, even though the host's own need may be far greater. And doing all of these things before you have asked for the stranger's name or religion, and not to expect or want anything in return.

Had I ever offered this? Did I know of anyone in England who could say they had done these things? *No.*

The weather changed. No more the beautiful morning sunshine, it was cold and raining heavily.

1 December, my birthday; where had the years gone? Today was my day off, and I was wondering how best to celebrate my birthday when I heard the front door opening.

'*Alo, cao Grem.*' I knew this voice.

'*Cao Stoja, kako ste vi?*'

Stoja entered the living room, looking fabulous and holding a large square cake, upon which were piped the words '*Sretan Rodjendan*'. She placed the cake onto the table and kissed me three times, this being the traditional Serbian greeting, then she gave me a firm hug.

Other voices now came.

'*Cao Grem,*' followed by giggles of laughter.

'*Yo! Cao Gavro,*' said a deeper voice.

Milka, Rada and Dusan now entered the room, each holding a gift wrapped in coloured foil paper.

Dusan opened a bottled of red wine and quickly filled four glasses. Stoja raised hers.

'*Sretan rodjendan Grem,*' she said, quickly repeated by the others.

'*Hvala lijepo,*' I replied. I turned to Milka. 'How did you know it was my birthday?'

'You told my mother at the barbecue when you arrived in Brčko; she remembers everything!'

I looked at Stoja and quietly said, 'Thank you'. She coyly dropped her eyes and shrugged her shoulders as if to say 'It was nothing'; to me, however, it meant a lot.

Then, as quickly as they had come, they left.

I had arranged to meet Dragan and Niko in the Galaxy bar and asked Bob to give me a lift into town.

'We should buy a local car to run about in, rather than using our UN vehicles,' I suggested.

'Good idea; see if your local friends can get us one and we could split the costs,' he replied.

He dropped me off and I walked inside.

'*Cao Gavro! Cao Gavro! Cao Gavro!*' came voices from all directions.

'*Kume! Sretan rodjendan,*' called Niko.

'Thank you, Niko; it seems that the whole bar knows it is my birthday!'

Drako, the bar owner, gestured for me to join him by the catwalk. There at the far end was a cooked pig's head mounted upon a silver tray, and plates of bread and roasted pork had been placed in each of the sitting booths. '*Samo za tebe Gavro, sretan rodjendan,*' he said.

This was a birthday gift for me!

'OOPAH!' Up went the cry, as loud music now blasted from the speakers and people crammed themselves into the sitting booths.

It was not long before the bar was packed with partygoers, both local and international. In Brčko, any excuse for a party just had to be good news.

I was moved by the kindness and generosities afforded to me by the local people; their actions were given freely, without the expectation of reward. Those who have nothing give everything, and I wanted to thank my local friends in a way that only they would understand and appreciate; after all, Christmas was now only two weeks away. The answer was to be shown to me on local television.

Enjoying a moment of peace and solitude, I turned on the television and flicked through the channels. One of the local TV companies had set up shop in the town of Bijeljina and was broadcasting a show from the Motel Ristić. Finely dressed people sat at long tables, being served a sumptuous meal by smartly dressed waiters. A live band played and people danced; everyone appeared to be having the most wonderful of evenings.

I quickly put on a change of clothes, climbed into our newly acquired 'Bosna-Car' and drove to the Galaxy bar.

The usual crowd was sat in one of the booths, and I joined them. The guys were drinking the usual local beer, while the girls sat drinking fruit tea or hot chocolate, the latter being so thick that a metal spoon could stand in it unaided. Niko was play fighting with Milan's girlfriend, Sladjana, who had just palmed his disposable lighter and substituted her own in its place, hers having run out of fuel.

'OK, people, what can you tell me about the Motel Ristić?'

'Only that it is one of the most expensive hotels in the RS; everyone would like to go there. Why do you ask?' said Sladjana.

'Because I am going to take you all there on Saturday; this will be my Christmas gift to you all,' I announced.

'You must be crazy, but thanks. How many do you intend to invite?' asked Dragan.

'Including Stoja and Dusan, my list stands at nineteen,' I replied.

On Saturday night, I collected Stoja and Dusan and met up with the rest of the gang at the Galaxy. After one quick drink, we headed off in convoy to drive the 30 kilometres to Bijeljina, a large town on the border with Serbia.

Driving into the car park, I caught my first sight of the hotel. It was big, lit with a large blue and red neon sign that proudly displayed the name 'Motel Ristić'. The large glass frontage and marbled floor shouted its high-class status.

As we entered the foyer, the head waiter scurried across. Dragan spoke to him. '*Gospodin Djokic, ja želim sto za devetnaest molim!*'

This caused an instant flurry of activity as tables were moved and cutlery reset, I gestured for Dragan to join me at the bar while the others took their seats.

'Dragan, do you think that 600 marks will cover the cost of food and wine?'

'Mate, to these people that is three months' wages; of course it will!'

'OK, then, here is the money; will you take care of everything?

'Yes, of course; just watch this, mate!'

47

We rejoined the others. A waiter slithered across the floor and faced Dragan, pen and notepad in one hand and a silver tray in the other.

Dragan ordered 12 bottles of wine, a variety of cooked meats and an assortment of the best vegetables, then dropped 400 marks onto the waiter's tray, telling him to return when the money had been spent.

A line of waiters scurried back and forth like a trail of ants, bringing large platters of cooked meat and wine. My friends were being treated like royalty. Even the singer thought someone famous had entered the hotel and danced her way over to the table to serenade Dragan.

It was at this point that I noticed the television screens located in each corner of the room and a cameraman wandering about, filming our group.

'Look, we are on TV!' I said, and everyone applauded and waved into the camera lens, knowing full well that friends and relatives would be watching the program back in Brčko.

The local people of all ages loved Serbian folk music; its simple but steady beat ensured that everyone would dance at some point of the evening. The dancing was normally started by the womenfolk; they would link hands behind the person standing next to them and form a ring around the room. The rhythm of the music would start slowly at first as the chain of women took two steps to the left, then two to the right, back to the left and then grapevine four paces right. This would cause the chain to slowly but steadily move around the room. The excitement would rise as the beat quickened, and before too long the women would be moving around the room at a phenomenal pace, only ceasing at the final beat of the drum, at which the ladies would return to their seats, exhausted but happy.

We never did spend all the money, but a great night was had by all.

It was cold, bitterly cold. Christmas Eve had arrived, and I was working the last of my night duties; tomorrow would see the start of the festive holiday period.

Snow had fallen heavily during the day, and the night frost caused the snow to crunch loudly with every step I took. Walking up the steps to the local police station, I stopped by the entrance door. Glancing across to the thermometer that hung on the wall told me that the temperature had dropped to −22 degrees. I shivered as the chill of the air ate through my clothing and stabbed at my body.

Srecko, my language assistant for the shift, came out of the duty office and walked towards me. Police officers crossed our path and got into waiting cars.

'Good evening, Srecko; what is going on?'

'We have to go the cemetery,' he replied.

We climbed into my 4x4 and followed the police at an unhurried pace through the town and down towards the river. A single-track road led to an isolated cemetery, about the size of a football pitch and surrounded by a rusty wrought-iron fence. All the vehicles parked outside the entrance gate, and, with the aid of torches, we entered on foot.

'What are we looking for?' I asked.

'Maybe a body; someone reported hearing gunshots coming from the cemetery,' replied Srecko.

The police officers spread out across the mass of graves. The light of the moon reflected off the surface of the snow, only to descend into pitch-blackness as clouds drifted across the starlit sky. The air was still, and the only sound to be heard was the crunching of the snow as we all moved about the headstones that lay before us. I passed the beam of my torch from one grave to another, being careful about where I placed my feet, as it was not uncommon for graveyards to be mined.

I heard a shout, and the flashing on and off of a torch guided me through the graveyard to reveal the saddest of scenes.

There, propped up against a headstone, sat a woman in her late thirties, dressed in tatty clothes that more suited a summer's day than the −20 degrees that I knew it to be. A single shot to the head had snuffed out her life, while in her arms, resting across her lap, lay the lifeless body of her small son.

The letters and photographs that lay strewn over the grave helped to give some explanation for why the two of them lay at the grave. For this was the grave of the dead woman's husband, who had been killed during the conflict some seven years earlier: a Serbian soldier, who probably thought he was fighting for a just cause, protecting his home and his family. A Serbian soldier, who was regarded by the rest of the world as a murdering, barbaric thug and not a caring, loving family man.

Yes, many Muslims had died, needlessly died, but this was not a time to continue the hatred; many Serbs had suffered the same fate, and at what point do you say, 'forgive the sins of mankind' and move onward towards peace? Punish not the man who pulls the trigger; punish the men who ordered him to do it.

This woman, since the death of her husband, had lived in a derelict house. She had no job, no money and no one to care for her, and she had given all and had nothing left to give. For her, happiness was being with her husband and son, and for now, in spirit at least, she had found that happiness again.

Dragan was right: this was the silly season. Those with family or friends could celebrate the festive period, but, for those without, Christmas would be such a depressing time of year. Each and every day revealed another victim of suicide somewhere in Bosnia.

The crime police now attended the scene and took over the investigation. Srecko and I returned to the police station. The rest of the duty passed without incident, so in the early hours of the morning we spent the time having a snowball fight. OK, it was childish, but it took our minds off those sadder, more distressing moments.

I woke up early; a glance across at the alarm clock that stood upon the bedside cabinet told me it was 9.32am. Normally after a night shift I would sleep through until 1.00pm.

I sat up in bed and saw my breath condense in the cold air; it was freezing cold inside the house. 'Damn, the heating has packed up!' I cursed.

I decided that the quickest way to get warmth was to dive under the shower. 'Yes, hot water would do the trick,' I muttered as I walked to the bathroom.

Naked and shivering, I stood in the bath and flicked over the lever to turn on the shower.

It hissed at me like an angry snake. A single droplet of freezing water formed itself around the showerhead, defying the rules of gravity until I leant forward to turn off the tap, and then it released its grip and slammed onto my shoulder to run down my spine. My teeth gritted and my back arched against the stab of cold water, and my mind cursed the perfect timing of a substance that had no comprehension of life.

I gave up on this idea and returned to the bedroom to dress quickly.

Wrapping a duvet around my body, I shuffled along the corridor and went upstairs. Bob and Wayne were dressed in similar fashion.

'It's a power cut, and my language assistant tells me they last for days at a time,' Bob said through chattering teeth.

'The weather men reckon it will drop to −30 tonight!' added Wayne.

51

'God, we will freeze to death in this climate!' I protested.

Bob remembered that he had a hexamine cooker in his kit bag and quickly set about the task of making coffee. I eagerly clutched at the hot mug, but my shivering caused the hot coffee to slop over the sides and burnt my fingers.

Bob lit a candle and placed it on the table in front of me. We laughed at this, as it made no difference to the room temperature whatsoever, but it did give a sense of warmth. Then the candle flickered and went out.

'Well, that is just great; it is so cold even the damn candle won't stay alight!'

I heard the front door opening. '*Alo, cao Grem*,' came the call.

'*Cao Stoja*,' I replied, shuffling my way downstairs.

'*Majka moj, hajde moj kuce, brzo*!' she said, and, after a warming hug, she gestured for us all to go with her.

Arriving at Stoja's front door, we removed our shoes, this being both polite and traditional.

I stepped into the hallway and the heat hit me with a welcome blast. Like us, they were without electricity, but they did have a wood-burning stove, and from this came the mouth-watering smell of dinner cooking.

'Guys, we must buy one of these, and very quickly!' I suggested.

Stoja set about the task of laying the table for her newly thawed guests, and Dusan passed around glasses of Rakija. '*Zivili*,' he said, and we returned the toast. A flush of heat began rising from the stomach to my chest, as the fiery spirit mixed with the natural juices of my belly.

Pork, roast chicken and vegetables were then served, all of which were washed down with copious amounts of red wine. I felt sated and content and could have happily spent the rest of my time on the sofa, laughing and joking with Stoja and her family.

Christmas saw the Muslim festival of Ramadan draw to a close. The period of fasting was over and now it was their turn to celebrate, and they certainly did party.

In Brčko, the average family lived on 200 marks per month; fireworks were a luxury that few could afford, so improvisation was the order of the day! At midnight, in the predominately Muslim areas across the town, the heavens opened up to the sound of gunfire as tracer bullets streaked across the clear night sky.

This was Christmas Day, so what was New Year's 2000 going to be like?

In the still night air, the sound of music and singing could be heard right across the town. I had already booked my place at the New Year's Eve party at the Galaxy bar; it was an excuse to dress up smartly.

I arrived early; thirty minutes later Dragan and Niko walked in, shortly followed by Milan, Sladjana and her sister. The bar had been dressed in festive style, festooned with flashing lights and paper chains that hung from the ceiling. Windows had been sprayed with imitation frosting and bottles of sparkling wine placed upon every table.

My thoughts returned to England and my daughter Lindsey. How I wished that she were here with me now to share in this memorable evening. It mattered not who you were or where in the world you were; everybody would remember how they celebrated the new millennium.

Soon the bar filled with people, all drinking and laughing. Music was playing loudly and people danced wherever they stood. All were enjoying the moment.

Then the lights went out!

Surely not tonight, not on New Year's Eve? Alas, yes, it was a power cut! The bar staff quickly lit candles, music was supplied via a ghetto blaster powered by a car battery and the evening carried on as normal.

As if commanded by a greater authority, the power returned about 11.00pm. 'OOPAH!' we all cried, and music blasted loudly again through the speakers.

The hour approached and I, along with everyone else, counted down the seconds, *ten, nine, eight and seven...*

And, at the moment of change, everyone hugged and kissed and toasted in the new millennium to shouts of '*Sretna Nova Godina*!', then went outside the bar.

The noise was deafening; the sky was alight with orange tracer bullets from AK-47s being fired from the balconies of flats that stood all around us. I was surprised to see that so many people still possessed these high-powered automatic weapons of war.

Suddenly, *boom* as a blast grenade exploded on the disused rail-track! *Boom* exploded another, the shockwave hitting my body with a thud.

From the roof of a block of flats, two anti-tank rockets launched skywards and exploded with an almighty bang. I watched in awe as the sky lit up better than any firework could achieve, but here lay the problem: as the saying tells us, 'what goes up must surely come down,' only this time what was coming down was hot molten metal!

I have never seen so many people squeeze through a three-foot doorway in such a short space of time, but they did. This was not a moment to mess around with such polite pleasantries as 'After you, madam; allow me to open the door for you; no, I insist.' Sod that! I made quite sure that I was the first to get back inside.

Back in the safe protection of the bar, the party carried on into the early hours. I had spent a most wonderful evening, and in one week's time I would get to repeat it, because one week later it would be the Serbian Orthodox Christmas.

The whole of January was one continuous party. It was customary to celebrate the season in whatever style took your fancy. Bob spent the period with Govinda to sample the Buddist celebrations, Wayne had returned to England to spend the festive season with his wife and family, Gill was mixing it with the Russians and Americans, and I chose to party with the Germans and locals. Each contingent held a party at some point, and it was a great way of meeting your international colleagues socially.

It was from such a party that I was walking home when I saw that local people were entering the Orthodox church. A strange time to go to church, I thought, considering it was ten o'clock at night.

Remembering Dragan's words, I chose to go inside and see for myself. Entering through the large oak doors, I could see rows of people standing, women on the left and men on the right. There are no pews in an Orthodox church.

I did not feel confident enough to venture too far inside and so stood by the entrance door. Viewing the painted murals that adorned the walls, I could see that each was of a saint, one of whom I immediately recognised. There he was, in his finest vestments of green and gold, and upon his white robe was the red cross of St George.

I looked closely at the other saints; here were St Peter, St Michael, St Nicholas and the Holy Mother. The Anglican church with whom I had been christened as a child celebrated all of these.

I did not want to intrude on the service and quietly slipped out of the door. Tanja, a language assistant, approached me.

'Hi, Gavro; are you going to church?'

'Not really; I didn't want to intrude.'

'Don't be silly, you are welcome here,' and she led me back inside.

The following day, I was at home when the phone rang.

'Hello, *molim*,' I said, unsure whether the caller was international or local.

'Hello, Grem, this is Rada; are you fine?'

'Yes, I am very fine, thank you; are you fine?' I said, slightly teasing her for her English.

'Yes, I am very fine, thank you,' she said with a giggle, then went on. 'My mother invites you, Bob and Wayne to Christmas dinner; will you come?'

'Yes, of course we will.'

'OK then, come when you are ready,' she said, and she put down the phone.

I was about to call upstairs to Bob and Wayne when the phone rang again.

'Hello, *molim*.'

'Hello, Grem, this is Rada again; are you still fine?'

'Yes, I am still fine; are you still fine?'

'Yes, I am still very fine, thank you, but I forgot to say goodbye, so goodbye!'

'Goodbye, Rada,' and I laughed loudly.

The three of us left the house, and, after stopping off at the shop to buy a bouquet of flowers for Stoja and a bottle of whiskey for Dusan, we continued on to their home. There I ate the most wonderful meal and got very drunk, as did everybody, but I enjoyed every second.

14 January was the Orthodox New Year and was strictly a Serbian affair; it was at this time that the giving of gifts was done, rather than Christmas Day. The Galaxy bar was once again prepared for a party, although I did not know this at the time.

During the day, I had driven to the UN office and left a small gift for all of the language assistants on the shift: nothing fancy, just a pen with the name of each recipient engraved upon it.

During the afternoon, Niko and Dragan called at the house and rang the doorbell. '*Cao kume, Srečna Nova Godina*,' they both said.

'*Vijeslava Christo*,' I replied, thinking I had got the formal reply correct.

Dragan and Niko both laughed. 'Good try, mate, but it needs work!' said Dragan, as he handed a gift to me.

I opened the wrapping and inside found a beautiful gold necklace from which hung a gold pendant in the form of a double-headed eagle sporting a crown upon its head. I knew that this had cost a small fortune. 'Thank you, Dragan; this will remain special to me'

'No, mate, thank you. I have been a language assistant for four years, and never has anyone done what you did today. We all thank you'.

I did not know what to say, so I picked up my coat and we all headed for the Galaxy.

The bar was busy, but only contained local people; a man stood beside the door and turned away uninvited guests. A small dispute arose with the doorman and a group of internationals; the bar owner intervened and said, 'Sorry, lads, this is our night; no internationals tonight, please.'

'But he is an international!' said a frustrated American, pointing towards me.

'Tonight Gavro is our guest,' and then he closed the door.

Only now did I realise my privileged position and was thankful to be so respected by the local people that they chose to include me on this, their special night.

As before I danced, drank and ate food. The music this time was supplied by a local folk band made up of trumpets, accordion, double bass and a large bass drum. It was a great evening; sparkling wine was sprayed everywhere and women danced on the tables, cheered on by the men.

And I was the only non-local person to witness it.

'Oopah!' I shouted, along with the others.

CHAPTER 4

A NEW JOB

The party season was over; everyone concentrated his or her efforts on the job in hand.

The German, Irish, Spanish and Portuguese monitors had now left Brčko; they would later be replaced with new monitors. Gill, Bob, Wayne and myself were now regarded as the 'old hands', and each of us was appointed to a new, more senior position. Bob became the commander of A4 station; this suited his admin skills. Wayne, having been a traffic officer back in England, now took over the role of co-locator to the chief of traffic police. Gill was in charge of regional admin, and I became chief of community police projects.

Brčko was now reformed into a 'Special District'; this was to be a pilot model, created by the United Nations in an attempt to create a multi-ethnic society, led by multi-ethnic government bodies such as medical and social services, housing ministry, customs, utilities (electric, telephones and water), donor aid, locally elected council officials and law administration, to include the judiciary, courts and local police.

The fundamental rule for any town or country is the rule of law. Laws form the basic infrastructure of a democratic society; without them a country would simply descend into anarchy.

But laws must be applied and enforced, not imposed by the will of the government of the day. They must be fair and apply to all members of society regardless of position, status or religion. Enforcement of the will of a political leader is not law; it is a dictatorship and, as such, a human rights violation.

The Brčko District police removed all trace of Serbian identity from their uniforms; this meant that they had to perform their duties wearing a pair of blue trousers and a blue shirt.

For the officers already in the force, morale sank to an all-time low. They had no identity or insignia to relate to. Without a uniform to project their authority, they became the subject of ridicule, not only from the public but also from police colleagues elsewhere in the RS and Federation. For the next six months, they were to be retrained and re-educated and were to acquire new skills and abilities. But they also had to prove themselves to be a professional body of men and women; they were, after all, still expected to police the residents of Brčko District.

Little did they know that in a few short months they would become the envy of every other police division in Bosnia. Men and women from both the Muslim and Croat communities were encouraged to join the newly reformed police force; it was to be the first and only multi-ethnic force in the country. This pilot project had to succeed if the country was to move forward towards reintegration of the communities and ultimately peace and stability.

Keith, a British police inspector, had now joined the team, having previously worked in Sarajevo. He took up the post of Regional Commander IPTF Brčko District. His presence was a great asset, as it meant that the British team now occupied all of the senior IPTF positions and were better able to push through policies and training with little or no resistance.

I chose my team with great care and with Bob's selective recruitment techniques was able to create a good mix of twelve monitors from different countries. To this I added a team of eight language assistants who represented all three ethnicities.

The Bosnian war was a struggle between three ethnic groups: Muslim, Serbs and Croats. As a result of the conflict, entire communities packed up what belongings they could and either moved or were forced to move to safer parts of the country. The Serbs moved northeast, the Muslims went south and the Croats migrated north-by-northwest.

As a result of this huge transference of communities, housing became a major problem. The natural thing to do was to occupy a property that had been abandoned by its owner, and so all three ethnic groups did this. To legitimise this taking over of someone else's home, the occupant had to register his intent with the local housing commission for that area and obtain a 'temporary housing permit' for the house that he was living in.

However, the war had now been over for six years and families wanted to take back the homes that they had been forced to leave. Achieving this meant going to the housing commission and obtaining a court order to evict the occupants of their homes.

The problem was this: where do the occupants go if there is no available housing?

The Deputy Supervisor United Nations Bosnia made a ruling that, in Brčko District, only those occupants who had liveable property elsewhere in the country would be subject to eviction, thus ensuring that no family was evicted out onto the streets.

This was a distressing period, as Serbs did not want to live in areas that were now dominated by Muslims and Muslims did not want to live in Serbian-dominated areas.

The basic thought to keep in mind was the fact that before the war everyone lived together, so why not after? But wounds take time to heal and memories are not quickly forgotten.

The official body responsible for selecting those families that were to be evicted was called the Multi-Ethnic Housing Commission (MEHC). This body of men and women was made up of Serb, Muslim and Croat local government officials, and a perfectly correct arrangement it was.

But this was Bosnia and money or the offer of favours could speed through an application, meaning that innocent families were being evicted out onto the streets.

The UN mandate made it quite clear that I was to monitor the local police; I had no UN mandate to monitor a government body such as the MEHC, yet I felt that certain members of the MEHC were committing a human rights violation by this fraudulent activity.

I arranged a meeting with Keith, Bob, the local police chiefs and the deputy supervisor for the United Nations US ambassador Gary Matthews. The purpose of the meeting was to raise my suspicions and discuss a solution.

The US ambassador had the authority to dismiss from office any official found committing a wrongdoing, but to do that he had to have evidence, and getting the evidence was not going to be easy. Evictions were a very emotive subject; they had to be dealt with firmly, resolutely, but with empathy, and could very easily spark a riot, putting the local police and us in great danger.

It was agreed that, as the local police had to conduct a risk assessment prior to attending the eviction site, they should also attend the MEHC meeting when those families to be evicted were selected. This was perfect, because wherever the police went, I went to monitor them. Now I could get inside the heart of the MEHC.

I returned to the office to call together my team and allocate each member an 'area of responsibility' (AOR) within the district. They had to get to know the community leaders in their areas and work closely with them so that they would learn to trust and respect the local police and resolve any community issues. Then I asked the chief of uniformed police, Pero Duric, to appoint two officers to each of the patrol areas. These men and women would take on the role of community police officers and would get to know the people within the communities intimately.

Will, an American, filled the role of my deputy. He was an intelligent man with great physical presence, although I suspect that being a former special forces 'Green Beret' may have had something to do with this. He and I flicked through photocopies of the notices that had been sent to those families about to be evicted.

'Has anybody got a magnifying glass?' I asked those in the office.

Zjelko rummaged about in his desk drawer. 'I have,' he replied.

I slid my chair over to Will. 'Have a look at this and tell me what you think.'

Will studied the document with the magnifying glass, moving it back and forth to improve the focus. 'Mmmm, the writing on that section is different from the rest, and look here.'

I leaned over and peered through the glass lens.

'See that faint vertical line? That is the edge of a piece of paper that is covering the original writing underneath, then the whole document has been photocopied to look like the original!'

'Those were my thoughts as well, but what we need now is the original document and I do not think the MEHC will hand that over to us willingly.'

Will gazed out of the window at the florist's across the street. 'Dead right there, my friend; no, this calls for a more subtle approach,' he said, drumming his fingers on the windowsill, deep in thought.

'Dragan, here is some money; just pop over to that florist's and buy me a nice bunch of flowers and a box of chocolates, will you?'

'OK, Will, what do you have in mind?' I asked.

Will smiled. 'Bosses have secretaries and secretaries have access to files, and women love to be flattered!'

Dragan returned quickly, carrying a small but beautiful bouquet of flowers and a gold box of chocolates. 'I'm not doing that again; the whole town is laughing at me!'

'Don't exaggerate, Dragan, I saw at least two people not laughing at you,' I teased.

'No, I saw three,' added Sandra, seizing the moment to have a go at him.

Dragan did not like being teased in this way; it was not good for his macho image.

'As Scott's friend once said, I am going outside and may be quite a while!' announced Will in a pompous and comic style, as he strode out of the door.

He returned less than 30 minutes later, his fidelity intact.

'That was bloody quick; did you skip foreplay?'

Will laughed. 'That and the cigarette after!' he replied, and he produced a file of documents from his jacket pocket.

He quickly compared the original with my photocopy. 'Look at this; the photocopy states that the occupant has liveable property in Bihać, but the original states that the property was destroyed during the war!'

I took the papers and compared the two. 'I wonder just how many eviction notices have been altered in this way.'

'At a rate of four evictions a day, five days a week, hell, we could be talking about a lot of families being thrown out onto the street,' said Will.

'OK, but this is only one piece of the puzzle; we need to collect more before we go to the ambassador,' I replied.

Each and every eviction notice was now studied in detail by either Will or myself and compared with the original documents, which Will somehow managed to continue furtively extracting from the MEHC offices. By the end of the second week, we had gathered enough evidence to present a case to the ambassador.

The evictions were suspended and, as a result of the investigation, one Serbian and two Croatian officials were dismissed from their posts. It did not make the job of supervising the evictions any easier or less dangerous, but it was a great result for human rights and won our department a lot of respect from the local police, the local community and other international agencies working in Brčko.

The snow melted away and heralded the beginnings of spring; the weather became warmer and colour came back to the town. Buildings still carried the scars of war and, for the people of Brčko District, life was still a constant struggle for survival.

Walking into the office, I gave the usual greeting. 'Morning, boys and girls.'

'Morning, Gavvers.' My mind registered an air of sadness in their voices.

Will entered the room, followed by Niko. 'Have they told you yet?' Will asked.

'No; told me what?'

'Niko's colleague has just lost his entire family to a car crash on the edge of town.'

I turned to Niko. 'I am sorry to hear that. Is there anything we can do to help your friend?'

'I do not know; what can be done when you lose your mother, father, wife and children?'

'There must be something. Come, let us go and talk to Pero.'

The entire building was silent; the waxy polish on the linoleum flooring caused the rubber soles of my boots to squeak as Dragan and I made our way to Pero's office.

His secretary sat at her typewriter, her slender fingers clicking away on the keys of the old machine. As the tears blurred her vision she would stop and wipe her eyes with a crumpled and shredded paper tissue.

Dragan pulled out a fresh tissue from his pocket and handed it to her. It seemed to me that he was always prepared for the unexpected.

'*Hvala puno,*' she said, and then she blew her nose.

'*Cao Gavro, kako si danas? Sedite molim,*' Pero called as he moved the black leather chairs and gestured for us to sit.

My local language skills were much improved now and I could easily make myself understood, but this was not a time for errors, so Dragan spoke without waiting for me; he knew instinctively what I wanted to say.

Pero explained that his officers had taken care of the welfare issues and funeral arrangements but asked if we would attend as international representatives. I said that we would.

It was dull and overcast as we drove to the officer's home in a small village on the Lončari road. I had not made any rules: those who chose to attend did; those who preferred not to stayed in the office.

Hundreds of people stood in the grounds of the officer's house; both he and his family were well liked and respected. This was indeed a tragic loss.

The officer, although heavily sedated to ease his suffering, shook my hand, though he did need to be physically supported by two of his closest friends.

But even I found it hard to fight back the tears as the two child-sized coffins were loaded onto the wooden cart next to the coffins of their mother and grandparents.

Will, Dragan, Beba and I returned to our vehicle and led the cortege behind the many hundreds of mourners who were walking behind the horse and cart that carried the coffins. A priest, holding a large brass crucifix, led the way to the cemetery.

Then Dragan spoke. 'Mate, can you stop? I would like to walk.'

'Yes, of course,' and I drew the vehicle to a gentle halt, causing the half-kilometre line of vehicles behind me to do the same.

Dragan got out. I could see the tears in his eyes.

'Are you OK? We don't have to do this.'

'I am OK,' he replied as he quietly closed the door.

Just as I was about to pull away, Beba leapt out of the 4x4 to walk alongside Dragan, linking her arm through his.

'Should we join them?' asked Will.

'No, let's just leave them alone.'

The cemetery to which we were heading was about two kilometres away, and as we slowly drove along I was amazed by the respect shown by the oncoming motorists. Each and every vehicle stopped, the occupants getting out and standing on the roadside; even buses pulled over and every fare-paying passenger got off the bus and paid their respects. I had never seen such a thing happen before and never saw it happen again in such magnitude.

When we arrived at the cemetery, all the coffins were placed into one large grave. It was fitting that they, having lived as a family, remained as such, even in death.

Everyone was affected by this day, and every week fresh flowers are placed at the scene of the accident, alongside five small wooden crosses.

As each day passed the mercury in the thermometer that hung on the police station wall rose higher and higher, and with the finer weather came a flood of travelling beggars. These were mainly of Albanian origin and, not having a work permit, turned the art of begging into a national business.

This morning, I diverted from my usual route to work to collect Beba from her apartment and saw families of Albanian beggars walking briskly towards the traffic light junction, heading towards town. The men were carrying crutches under their arms, the women adjusting their apparently heavily pregnant stomachs, and teams of young children were running about them.

Beba and I drew up to a halt at the traffic light junction. Instantly, one man went into action, sliding his arms into the crutches and limping across to our vehicle.

Feigning a war injury, the man tapped on the side window. '*Jedan mark, molim te,*' he asked.

'The man is just a crook; do not offer anything,' said Beba. 'He was walking fine five minutes ago!'

The beggar continued to tap on the window, then, when that failed, hobbled to the front of the vehicle to obstruct my path as the lights changed to green.

Berdump, berdump.

Beba howled with laughter. 'I think you ran over his foot! Well, at least he has crutches to use!'

I glanced into my rear-view mirror to see a very irate beggar jumping up and down and waving a crutch at me. 'Nothing seriously damaged there, I think!'

When we arrived at the police station, Will was sitting outside the café bar, enjoying a morning coffee. Beba and I joined him and ordered the same. It was so pleasant to sit and bask in the morning sunshine and provided a very relaxed start to the day.

By the time the coffee arrived, the beggar wives and children had started their morning of solicitations. It was the children who approached first, but they were quickly chased away by the waiter. '*Mrsc kuc! Mrsc kuc!*' he shouted, as he flicked a tea-towel at the bare legs of the grubby, unkempt child.

When this failed to extract the desired funds from those who chose to drink coffee *al fresco*, the mother commenced phase two. She shuffled her way over to our table, dressed in a long, dirty dress, her huge stomach giving the impression of being heavily pregnant, while in her left arm she carried a baby.

'*Jedan mark, molim te,*' she asked, and she held out her empty hand in the hope that I would fill it with cash.

'*Ne hvala,*' I replied, dismissing her request with a wave of the hand.

She now pinched the toe of the infant that she carried to make it cry, then turned to face Will. '*Jedan mark, molim, moj cerka gladan*!'

'What is she saying, Beba?'

'She is asking for one mark and saying that her daughter is hungry.'

Will took out his wallet. 'Sorry, but I only have a one hundred mark note; I do not have any change!'

Beba translated his words to the woman, at which she promptly pulled out a leather wallet stuffed full of notes and offered to give him change.

'Ma'am, if you have that much money, you have no need for mine; now go away!'

Dragan translated to the woman, adding a few local swear words to good effect. She shuffled off to the next table.

The woman remained in the same 'pregnant' state for two years, and is probably still allegedly pregnant; this must be a gestation record.

'Let's go for a walk around the marketplace,' suggested Will.

The marketplace was situated alongside a small relief river that ran into the river Sava. The route there was a short walk down the hill and over a small concrete bridge.

As we walked, Dragan saw a beggar on crutches, doing the usual war wound limp. He crept up behind him and made squeaking noises each time the man took a step. The man turned sharply and was about to hurl a mouthful of abuse, but saw Dragan's physical stature and chose instead to tuck his crutches under his arm and walk off at a brisk pace.

We all laughed, but my laughter was cut short by the sight of the people sitting on the floor of the bridge. About twenty men and women of all age groups sat on small blankets, each offering a grubby upturned hand and begging for money.

But these were not the con-merchants of earlier, these cases were genuine, and all were the victims of land mines. Each beggar had removed an item of clothing to reveal stumpy severed limbs, hands, arms, legs and feet, all bearing the grossly healed scar tissue that had formed over the wounds.

I wanted to look away, but found myself staring in morbid fascination. Brčko town was surrounded with minefields, and I was well aware of the dangers, but this was 'in your face' reality. These were not soldiers; these people were innocent victims who chose to walk through a field of long grass and paid a high price for doing so.

I wanted to give, but if I gave to one I would have to give to all, so, forgive me, Lord, I shamefully walked on.

Returning to the police station, I saw an elderly woman standing on the pavement. Although it was hot and sunny, she was wearing a heavy woollen coat and carpet slippers. In her hand she was holding three photos mounted on a piece of card, and she spoke to nobody.

'Dragan, why is that woman standing there?'

'Those photos are the death notices of her husband and two sons who died during the war. Her pride will forbid her to ask for charity, but, if you wish to give, just tuck some money into her jacket pocket and say nothing; that way you will not offend her pride.'

I immediately took a ten-mark note from my pocket, and, when I drew level with the woman, I discreetly tucked the note into her coat pocket and turned to walk away.

'*Hvala lijepo, Christo sa mnom, danas*' she said quietly.

My mind translated her words: 'Thank you very much; Christ is with me today.'

I hope that woman lives for many years to come.

Back in the office, Will and I discussed the merits of a project that Korinorr had suggested regarding the cleaning of water wells. Korinorr was a member of my team and came from Pakistan; he was very knowledgeable on such issues.

Suddenly my radio crackled into life. 'Charlie 4 Alpha from Charlie 42 urgent, over!'

It was Yvette, another member of my team, who was out supervising an eviction now that they had resumed. Her voice sounded frantic.

'Go ahead, Yvette; what is the problem?'

'Gavvers, I need you here at the site, things have gone really bad, there are about 200 angry people trying to stop this eviction. I think we are going to need SFOR and a hell of a lot more local police!'

'Understood, now get away from the site; I will contact Pero and join you soon as!'

My office emptied, with everyone dashing to their vehicles. I ran to Pero's office and asked him to send a squad to the village of Čelinac, then ran downstairs to join Will, who was waiting for me in the 4x4.

Arriving at the scene, we watched from the roadside as the local police placed a cordon of men around the house where the eviction was to take place.

The angry crowd, their numbers growing by the minute, was now hurling rocks and building rubble at the officers. Although the police had no insignia, the ethnicity of each officer was easily determined by his name, which was on a small plastic card that hung on his shirt. This demonstration was in a Serbian community, and the angry mob targeted, with ferocity, those officers of Muslim or Croat ethnicity.

Then a moment of magic occurred within the madness. The Serbian police officers pushed away the crowd and shielded their non-Serb colleagues, then every officer removed his name badge and linked arms with the colleague next to him. This was an amazing display of unified loyalty. Everyone stopped what they were doing, the area went deathly quiet and the crowd just stood in silence, looking at the police, who were sweating, bleeding, even trembling, but remained standing together with their guns securely fastened in their holsters.

One officer had been struck on the head by a rock and was feeling the effects of his injury; he started to buckle at the knees. His colleagues on either side pulled him upright and supported his entire body weight on their arms.

'Come on, let's give them water,' I said, remembering that I had six cases of water in the back of my truck.

My team deployed amongst the police, handing out the two-litre bottles of water and giving first aid to those who were injured. I ran over to the officer with the head wound, first aid kit in one hand and a bottle of water in the other.

We will be torn to shreds if this kicks off now, I thought to myself. This was indeed a very big risk.

As soon as the two officers released their grip on the injured man, he collapsed to the ground. Kneeling down beside him, I gave him water, then ripped open a head bandage and placed it on the wound, which was now bleeding heavily.

Niko left his position on the cordon and knelt down beside me. 'My friend, you must go; these people will kill you if you show feeling for a Muslim officer. I will care for him,' he said, with genuine concern on his face.

I turned and looked at the crowd with a certain degree of anxiety. I could feel my hands trembling.

'To hell with them; he is a policeman just like the rest of us!'

Other officers who were drinking the water now sat on the ground. Surprisingly, so did the crowd.

Then, slowly at first, two or three crowd members sat with the officers, who then shared the water. More crowd members followed, and everyone chatted as if they were old friends.

The scene was so surreal that, had I not been there to witness it, I would never have believed it.

A senior official from OHR arrived and spoke to the community leader, and an agreement was made to suspend the eviction for seven days pending an appeal.

The next week, the eviction took place, this time without incident or protest.

A new battle now started between the police and the local press, who were making allegations of excessive force and brutality during the incident, all of which were untrue and did nothing to enhance the reputation of the police. The police chiefs themselves did not help matters when they published counter allegations against the community. Back in my office, my team would report that things were not going well and that the communities were no longer talking to the police.

It was now that I had a most inspired idea. What the police force needed was a fully trained, professional press officer: a man who could act as a spokesperson and promote the force. My problem was going to be getting a police force that normally kept its activities a secret to open its doors and welcome the media.

'Chief Kokanovic will never go for it!' said Will.

'Then we will have to push him into a corner, and I know the two best men for the job!'

'Who?'

'You and Srecko!'

Will smiled; he knew that I had just named the two most intimidating men on the unit. 'You're not suggesting that we...?' He paused momentarily as I started to smile. 'Oh, I see, you are suggesting it! Come on, Srecko, let us go and have a shout at the police chief.'

It was not long before the sounds of a heated argument filled the corridor. People simply stood aghast and wondered who had dared to speak to the chief of police in this way. Kokanovic was 'old school'; to win his respect you had to be as hard as he was; otherwise he would simply walk all over you.

Will and Srecko came out of the chief's office. In the hall stood a four-foot-long folding table, and Will, with a face red with rage, picked this up and threw it out of the window into the street below.

I stepped back into my office. God, he has gone and lost the plot, I thought.

Srecko and Will entered and closed the door, and the pair then burst into laughter.

'Srecko, you were brilliant, the best bit of interpreting I have ever seen!' said Will.

'That was fun; can we go back and shout at him some more?' asked Srecko.

'OK, gents, but did he agree?' I asked.

'He is thinking about it and will send his secretary down here with his reply shortly.'

Minutes later, there came a knock at the door.

'Chief Kokanovic agrees to your plans and says you must train Mr Majstorovic in time for Madeline Albright's visit on Friday; you have three days. Oh, yes, can you please return my table from the street?' The secretary smiled and left.

By a stroke of good fortune, Will knew a colleague called Jim, who worked for an agency called ICITAP. Jim was skilled in the training of officials who gave briefings at congress meetings, and it was he whom Will now called on the telephone.

The training of Majstorovic went ahead at a blistering pace; he was taken to television studios for camera presentation techniques, then on to radio stations for interview training. Back in the office, Jim taught him the finer points of what to say and what not to say, how to avoid a question, how to dress and how to work an audience. In short, he turned a lawyer into a media star.

Madeline Albright's visit came and went without too much protesting from the local community, save for the odd egg being thrown, but it was tonight that Majstorovic was to prove his worth, as he was to present a live press briefing following Madeline's visit.

My team and I sat in our office, all glued to the TV screen. Would he do well? I wondered.

Into the briefing room strode Majstorovic, and he stepped up confidently to the rostrum. He delivered his part perfectly and was a credit to Brčko District police.

The following day, Chief Kokanovic came to the office and spoke to Will. Dragan translated his words. 'He thanks you for the training of Mr Majstorovic and asks if we could train him to do the same.'

'Life will not get any better than this!' I said.

The attitude of the community changed and became cooperative again. The team ensured that the local police received the credit for any projects done, and often TV crews would go out with the police and film the officers at work. Our projects were now receiving national attention and morale within the force was improving; however, the best was yet to come!

Korinorr had come to the end of his mission and was returning to his home in Pakistan. I needed to find a replacement.

I was pondering this issue when the telephone rang. It was Bob.

'Hello, mate; I have just had Govinda asking if he could apply to come onto your unit. What are your thoughts?'

'Why not? Korinorr leaves at the end of the month, and I do need a replacement quickly.'

Bob took care of the selection process, but to Govinda this appointment was an honour of the highest degree, as I was about to discover.

On his first morning I was a little late arriving at the office, having picked up three language assistants on my way in. Govinda stood outside the office door, looking smart in a freshly ironed uniform.

'Good morning, Govinda; welcome to the community police department!'

'Good morning, Mr Bavin, sir. I am thanking you most humbly for considering me worthy enough to join your office.' He smiled broadly, nodding his head from side to side and bowing repeatedly with his hands in the prayer position.

'Govinda, you have earned this appointment on your own merit; you are equal to anyone who enters this office, so please stop bowing and come inside.'

As the days passed, I found that Govinda was indeed the right man for the job; he was a fully committed member of the team, and as he settled in I came to know more about the man.

He told me that, back in his native country of Nepal, he was subject to the caste system. I did not understand the finer points of this, but basically your surname identified your caste and, as such, you could only aspire to a level in society that your caste would allow.

Govinda wanted desperately to be of equal status to that of his brother, who was an officer in the Gurkha regiment. To achieve this he needed to be promoted to the rank of police commander, and promotion could be accelerated if a recognised commendation were to be awarded to him for, say, bravery or some other similar distinction. All of this went some way to explaining why he was so dedicated to his job, which he did well.

I found him to be the most humble, loyal, polite and likeable man that I had ever met, but he would also drive me to distraction.

Govinda sat at his desk, typing his daily report, stabbing at the keyboard with one finger of each hand and making whining noises like a lost puppy each time he struck a wrong key. I gazed out of the window and smiled as I recalled my first attempts to use a computer, and then something caught my eye.

'Govinda, what is that large box in the rear of your pickup truck?'

'Oh, sir, I am buying a 80cm flat screen TV at very good cheap price from Arizona market!'

'You do understand that items sold at the Arizona market are either stolen or copied?'

'I am copying, sir.'

'No, Govinda, you misunderstand me; when I say copied, I mean copied as in fake, not real!'

His face contorted into a confused frown. 'I am buying not real TV?'

'Well, it may be real, but I am guessing that it is stolen!'

'But I am getting one year guarantee!'

'Govinda, when you and your TV return to Nepal in three months' time and your TV goes "pfutt", are you really intending to return to Bosnia to get it fixed?'

'Oh my God! Do you think it will be "pfutting", sir?'

'Probably not, but I suggest you go and take it home before those two beggars standing beside your vehicle decide to steal it!'

'OH MY GOD!' he shouted as he ran out of the office and along the corridor.

'Should I go with him?' asked Sandra, his language assistant.

'No, Sandra, you may as well go home for lunch; besides, he will be rushing back into the office in about ten seconds!'

'How can you possibly know that?'

'Simple: he has left his car keys on his desk!'

Govinda burst into the office and frantically rummaged about his desk. Sandra stood by the door and jingled his keys.

'I am thanking you so much, Sandra.'

'Good, then you can give me a lift home!'

Govinda ran back down the corridor as fast as his short little legs would carry him, slowly followed by Sandra, who just shook her head in disbelief.

CHAPTER 5

A CALL FROM THE AMBASSADOR

It sounded strange when Will suggested that we 'pop over' to Croatia for lunch. The thought of travelling to another country just to have a quick meal sounded extravagant in the extreme. But, in reality, lunch in Croatia was feasible by virtue of the fact that getting there was just a short drive over the iron bridge that spanned the river Sava.

The river formed a natural borderline and, once we had crossed, we were in Gunja: a small village, less than 200 metres inside the Croatian border and made up of a few houses and one lavish-looking German-style restaurant (the fact that the owner was German may have had some influence on this).

The contrast between the restaurants of Brčko and those of Croatia was quite profound. It brought to mind the phrase 'coming from the wrong side of the tracks', only here you would substitute the word 'river' for 'tracks'. On the Bosnian side, meals were basic, limited to a choice of pork or lamb, but in Croatia the menu could offer a huge variety of steaks, fish and roasted meats, all served with a wide variety of freshest vegetables. It seemed to demonstrate the difference between the low-paid, communist life of the Bosnian and the wealthy, democratic lifestyle of the Croatian. Remember that both were once part of the former Yugoslavia.

Our meal cost 60 marks each, and that included wine and dessert. Back in the UK that would be a very inexpensive meal, but to a Bosnian that was a week's wages lavished on food. Needless to say, not many Bosnians would attend here, but then I doubted that they would want to.

Back in the office, Will gathered together the daily reports from the other team members. We were about to hold a meeting to discuss which projects were feasible when the telephone rang; it was Penny, the PA to the US ambassador.

'Hi, Penny. We have not seen you for ages; where have you been?' I assumed the call to be a social one.

'Well, hi, honey, I have spent the week in Budapest, but listen: the ambassador would like to see you and Will. Can you come to the office straight away, as he must leave for Sarajevo this afternoon?' Penny was from Texas, and the way she spoke was almost musical.

I told her that we would, so Will and I left the office and headed for the OHR building.

Upon arriving at the building, we were escorted by an armed protection officer to the ambassador's office. Penny was sat at her desk, typing a memo, but on seeing us arrive she stood up and hugged us both. 'So how are my two most hunky IPTF men?'

She did not wait for an answer; instead, she opened the office door and announced our arrival to Gary Matthews, the US ambassador and deputy supervisor to the UN in Bosnia.

Gary stood up from behind his large oak desk. He was a giant of a man, who stood at least seven feet tall, yet his stature was not intimidating; he was a warm and welcoming man who spoke in a soft, refined American accent.

'Sorry to drag you guys over here, but I am in need of your skills. I am going to be singing your praises this afternoon in Sarajevo, but I'd like to ask for your assistance with two further projects.'

Will and I relaxed; projects were something we could handle.

The ambassador went on to explain that the legal office were writing the new laws for the country, to be referred to as the 'book of rules', a portion of which related to the local police. 'I would like you to read it and add or amend any part that you feel should be rewritten; just make short comments in the margins. However, the book should be treated as secret for now and I would like to have it back by Tuesday.'

Will drew the large bundle of documents towards him. 'I guess this is going to be my job!' he said.

I knew why we were being asked to do this. Jim from ICITAP had spent many months of devoted hard work creating the 'policy manual'; this was to be the authority from which the local police were to derive their operational powers and which formed the basis for the rule of law that would apply throughout the whole of Bosnia. Contained within the policy manual was the 'book of rules', and this part had been created by an American police officer who, sadly, thought highly of himself and sought to create his own empire, figuratively speaking, that is. His own arrogance created conflict between Jim and other senior officials at OHR and caused the delay of the policy manual's implementation. For some strange reason, he felt that the policy manual was a totally unnecessary document and refused to co-operatively assist in the creation of the book.

The ambassador was far more aware of politics and knew that the policy manual was the most important document for the local police: it directed the authority to the 'book of rules'; one was useless without the other. He had called us in to resolve the issue. (For the record, every canton within Bosnia now uses the policy manual.)

'And the second project, sir?' I asked.

'The Brčko District police are soon to finish their probationary period and will be sworn in as the country's first multi-ethnic police force. I would like you to design and create a new police uniform and multi-ethnic insignia, to include badges of rank.'

'I cannot foresee any difficulties with that,' I quipped.

'It will not be as easy as you think, Graham; it took this country four years just to agree on a national flag! Your design must comply with this list of conditions and win the approval of the Bosnian parliament, the RS ministry and the United Nations, not forgetting the local police themselves, of course, and you only have two months to achieve all of this!'

Penny now entered the room, carrying a tray of coffee and biscuits. As usual, her timing was perfect, but I guess that is the difference between good and excellent personal assistants.

Our cue to leave was indicated by the arrival of an armed protection officer, who escorted us back to the reception area of the building.

Will's next comment decided our plan of action. 'I will sit and read and you can sit and create a masterpiece!'

Little did I realise just how late a night we were about to have.

The office was empty; all the staff had finished for the day. Will and I walked in and sat down; he read while I got on with the task of drawing a variety of insignia.

The ambassador was right; this was not as easy as I had first thought. Each time I came up with an idea, Will would say something like 'too religious', 'too military' or 'too ethnic'.

Frustration was getting to me, so I wrote down on the flip chart the list of conditions that the Ambassador had given to me:

1) *The design must not offend any ethnicity or religion.*
2) *It must represent Bosnia and Brčko District.*
3) *It must identify the person as a police officer.*
4) *Any writing must be in both Cyrillic and Latin script.*

5) *It must be nationally approved and have a defined meaning.*

'Fancy a beer, Will?'

'Good idea!'

On my return to the office about an hour later, ideas came flooding into my mind. By 2.00am I had the rough sketches of two designs that complied with all the conditions, and even Will could not find any part objectionable.

The office door opened; it was Dragan. 'Hello, mate; why are you both still here?'

'Reading and drawing; what made you come here?'

'I saw the light on.'

I showed Dragan the designs that I had prepared. He took off his coat and sat down at a computer.

'They would look better if done on the computer!' he said, and he opened an image editing program and copied my designs. They did indeed look more professional. 'We will show these to Chief Kokanovic on Monday and see which one he prefers.'

The following week, Kokanovic reported back that he liked both designs and suggested that one be used for the cap badge and the other as the uniform insignia. This made good sense, so both designs were submitted for approval to the ambassador, who in turn sent them off to UN headquarters in Sarajevo.

By the end of the month, we had received instructions to arrange for the manufacture of the shields and insignia. We achieved this by contacting a company in Belgrade who produced identity shields for the Yugoslavian military and police. A local firm would make the cotton-stitched insignia, and, with a certain degree of negotiation, also agreed to make the rank badges. A trip to Banja Luka found a manufacturer of leather goods, who by a strange coincidence was the cousin of one of my language assistants; he was given the task of producing the leather wallet that contained the police shield. Finally, as a gift to Brčko police, my office raised the funds to have transfers made, and these were to be fitted to all of the police vehicles.

The swearing in of the police officers was to be a moment of history; for the first time in Bosnia, a multi-ethnic police force would come to formally exist.

Will was determined that this day would be a momentous occasion for the officers of the local police; it was, after all, their day. They had worked and trained hard, but what was more significant was the fact that they had done it as a team from differing ethnic backgrounds. It had been only six years since the country had been at war!

The local football stadium was chosen for the venue and invitations sent to every government minister and senior official. Ensuring their safety was going to prove to be a security nightmare; if anybody had intentions of wiping out the entire Bosnian leadership, along with UN ambassadors, then this was the place to do it. I was glad to hand over the mantle of responsibility to Will; his vast experience of 'close protection' and 'security risk assessment' made him the right man for the task in hand, although I doubt that he would thank me for giving him the job.

I could only stand and watch as Will spent many late nights with the local police anti-terrorist squads, training them in individual protection principles and getting the local officers to change the communist mindset of 'crowd control' protocols. Working together with Rich, a former Navy SEAL and now the ambassador's protection chief, Will ensured maximum security of the site during the ceremony.

On a hot summer's day, 300 men and women of the Brčko multi-ethnic police force paraded in front of their country's political leaders, along with Ambassador Matthews, SRG Klien, Brčko District Mayor Kisic, Jim

Lyons from ICITAP and representatives from every canton in Bosnia.

It was fitting that the first officers to receive their new shields were a female officer and three male colleagues, one of each ethnic background.

The local police of Brčko now received local, national and international recognition for their effort and dedication, aided by global TV coverage from CNN.

So what was the big bonus? The officers' pay; this was increased from 240 marks a month to 900. They were not only a very professional body of men and women but were now the highest paid, and they deserved it!

CHAPTER 6

THE WORD OF THE DAY IS 'IMPLEMENTATION'

Dragan and I stood in the entrance hall of the police station chatting to a group of local police officers about the 'swearing in' ceremony.

Two senior police chiefs from the Federation side and two RS police chiefs had come to see Chief Kokanovic, more out of curiosity than anything else, and Pero Duric was showing off the new uniform and insignia of the Brčko District police. He did look smart in his light blue shirt with gold embroidered epaulets and was obviously proud of his new appearance.

Morale within the force was at a new high; there seemed to be a buzz that filled every office, and the officers themselves were enjoying all the media attention that was now being focused upon them. I, too, felt a sense of achievement and was proud to have played a part in this notable change.

Then Dragan tapped me on the arm and pointed to a dishevelled-looking teenage girl who had just walked past and was now talking to the duty officer through the small glass hatch. He had sensed something was wrong and had eavesdropped on her conversation. 'She is saying that she has been raped by her stepfather.'

Tears now fell from the girl's face as she spoke, and Dragan placed a comforting arm around her shoulders and gave her words of reassurance.

I was curious as to how they were going to deal with such a sensitive issue as this. If the local police had any areas of weakness, then the two most notable were domestic violence and child abuse, although this was not surprising, as ten years ago the UK police had not handled these two issues too well either. Here, the officers lacked empathy; everything had to be dealt with in a cold and matter-of-fact way.

It appeared that the girl had reported similar incidents two years earlier, but the matter had not been dealt with. Now she was marched from office to office, each time being asked to recount her allegation.

In the afternoon, she was taken to the hospital to be examined, after which she was handed over to the social services, who sent her home, presumably to live with the man who had committed the violation. This did not sit well with me. I was forced to accept that the local police had performed their duty, given the limited resources and funding, but there had to be a better solution.

Returning to the office, I gathered together the team. I had decided that the best way forward was to create a 'safe house' within Brčko District: a place where the victim could be taken and where, rather than having the victim go to all the different agencies that would be involved, the agencies could visit the victim, thus reducing further trauma.

However, to achieve my goal I had to overcome three fundamental problems: where to find a suitable government-owned property, how to fund the project and finding the highly qualified staff who would train the police to become skilled investigators in these sensitive crimes.

My team moved into top gear. Will contacted his American colleague who worked for ICITAP, the International Criminal Investigative Training Assistance Program, to assist in the training of the police. The rest of the team deployed amongst the people and spoke to community leaders, trying to find a suitable site. I arranged meetings with the town's leader, Mayor Kisic, to see what funding could be offered and to win over the town's council in order to gain support for the project.

It was Will who reported back first. 'Jim from ICITAP has agreed to train the forensic officers, and Ambassador Matthews will talk to Madeline Reese, the head of OHCHR, to see what assistance she can offer.' The ball was now starting to roll and progress was being made.

The following morning, I could hear the telephone ringing as I unlocked the office door. Beba answered the call.

'It is Madeline Reese from OHCHR,' she said, and she transferred the call to my desk.

The conversation was short and to the point: would I go to Sarajevo and meet her at her office at 10.00am on Wednesday to discuss the project? She added that she had some information that would greatly assist me; this I found intriguing.

The telephone rang again; Branka answered the call and wrote down a message, which she slid over to Will.

'Mayor Kisic wants to see us; when will we be available?' he asked.

'Let's go now!' I suggested.

We took Dragan and Beba with us; if this was to be a long and in-depth meeting, it would be easier for the language assistants to share the translation.

As with any municipal building, crowds of people were wandering about, going to this office or that department. Down the entire length of the staircase stood people who were submitting forms to have their homes returned. The hot, humid atmosphere caused them to wave their papers in an effort to move the air and cool down. They were in for a long wait.

I politely pushed my way past these people; the others followed in single file.

Leather padded doors were obviously the fashion in communist political circles, and the door to Mayor Kisic's office was no different, although it was larger than any other door in the building. Kisic was a big man, in both stature and position; he wielded a lot of political clout within Brčko but always toed the party line as dictated by those at party HQ in Banja Luka.

Our meeting was to follow the well-rehearsed rules of Serbian business etiquette: a cigarette, coffee and a 15-minute chat about the merits of rosewood for constructing his boardroom table, and then it was down to business.

'So, Mr Gavro, you are seeking a state-owned property to use as a safe-house?'

'Yes; ideally I would like it to be rent-free and have rooms that could be turned into temporary living accommodation.'

'Nothing is free in this world, Gavro; we must assist each other if we are to make progress.'

'What is it that you need?'

'If I am to provide such a building, donor aid will have to provide funds to refurbish it; the ministry does not have the budget to do this.'

'I will not make a promise that I cannot keep, but I will speak to the ambassador to see if he will release funds for the project.'

Kisic pushed a button that was attached to the table; this was obviously to summon someone waiting outside, as in walked a short, bespectacled man. 'Gavro, may I introduce Dr Anton Domic, head of social services? He will show you a property that we think will suit your needs.'

Anton explained that an ambulance station in the Federation side of the district had been rebuilt by US aid, although the interior would need to be finished off. He then suggested that we leave straight away to go and view the site.

The route to the ambulance station was going to take us a good 20 minutes of driving; the problem was not the distance but the state of the single-width road upon which we drove. Large potholes and rocks caused the 4X4 to roll from one side to the other like a ship in a force ten gale, and I wondered if a normal car would be able to make this journey. My doubts were quickly dismissed, though, because the very next moment a battered-looking car came chugging past in the opposite direction, the rear seats completely filled to the roof with cabbages.

The road ahead was now a dust cloud, caused by the passing car, and driving was achieved more by luck than judgement.

On entering a small village of around 15 houses, I pulled in and drove down a gravel drive, which led behind the only café bar. Here was sited the ambulance station: a two-storey construction, made of brick and with white cement-rendered walls.

Inside, I was shown white tiled examination rooms and, further along the corridor, smaller rooms that would ideally be used as offices. A spiral staircase led me to the first floor; this was the living area and comprised three bedrooms, a living room with a kitchen to one side and, along the hall, a bathroom with shower and toilet.

This property was far better than I could have hoped for; it was perfect, and I knew that the cost to complete the refurbishment would not break the bank.

I thanked Dr Domic and returned to the office. Phase one of the project was 'in the bag', as they say.

It rained heavily as Will and I prepared for the trip to Sarajevo. This time we were taking Beba and Zjelko to act as our language assistants.

There was no short cut to Sarajevo; whichever way you went, you had to go through the mountains. Bosnian roads and water did not go together well, and the worn, smooth surface of the tarmac ensured that you paid careful attention to the road ahead. Careless neglect would easily find you crashing to the bottom of a ravine, as many a wrecked vehicle that now lay rusting away bore witness. Will and I tossed a coin to decide who was going to drive; Will lost.

Back in the UK, a journey of 140 kilometres would have been a short hop down the motorway, but in Bosnia the trip was to take us three hours. This was basically due to those farmers who seemed determined to shift an entire load of sweetcorn stalks in one go and, as a result, created an impassable mountain on wheels.

Arriving at the tall blue UN building with only minutes to spare, we walked at a brisk pace through the corridors of power.

Madeline was at her desk, sending e-mails to all corners of the globe. 'Hello, Graham, Will. Please come in and take a seat; I just need to make a quick phone call to the person I want you to meet.'

She made the call and invited us to go to the cafeteria downstairs, where we could relax and talk. There I was introduced to the head of a local NGO called 'Medica Zenica', a group that specifically dealt with domestic violence and child abuse within Bosnia. 'Margarita' (not her real name) had written a book called *Drugi Put*, which described the pilot program that she and her team had created to deal with domestic violence. The team at Medica Zenica were well informed and skilled in counselling those women who had suffered since the war years and would prove to be a vital asset in training the local police in skills that to date they were lacking.

Madeline and 'Margarita' were very interested in our project, and the following week they flew up to Brčko via UN helicopter to view the facilities that we had now acquired.

The project was gathering pace. In a restaurant in the middle of town, I introduced Madeline and the team from

Medica Zenica to the agencies that would be involved in the use of the facility. These would include such people as the police, social services, gynaecologists and other doctors from the hospital, forensic scientists and representatives who specialised in family issues from an aid agency called World Vision.

The project would take time to implement fully, and time was not on my side, as my mission would finish in a few months, but for now at least the seeds were sown.

The temperature soared into the hundreds; it was a time for women to wander about with the bare minimum of clothing, and each and every Saturday a wedding party would celebrate the occasion by driving around the town, honking their car horns and waving to members of the public. An air of happiness filled the senses.

It was the hissing of the showerhead that alerted me to the fact that there was no water in the house. I telephoned Stoja to let her know the situation and she said that, due to the hot weather, the well would have run dry, but not to worry; she would resolve the issue.

To my surprise, a fire truck pulled up outside the house an hour later and four firemen laid a hose from the truck to the well in order to pump 6000 gallons of water into it.

It did not take long to realise where the water had come from, for the moment I turned on the tap the brackish smell of wet cardboard and rotted wood was unmistakable. This was water that had been drawn from the River Sava, and once the brown sediment had settled it was OK to use for washing and flushing the toilet.

Water had always been one of the major issues in Brčko; while the town centre did have the benefit of a main water system, those homes on the outskirts had to rely on wells that had been dug in the rear garden. Not that the town centre was immune to supply problems; they, too, often went long periods without this essential fluid due to the failure of the poorly-maintained water pumps at the pumping station.

It was an Italian NGO called 'Proni' that chose to tackle this problem; it laid a pipeline from the town of Bijeljina to Brčko and installed new and powerful pumps at the pumping station.

The moment had come for the new pumps to be switched on, and we all waited in excited anticipation. All seemed to go well until I drove into the town centre, for there, in the middle of every street, children played, darting in and out of the fountains of water that shot some ten feet into the air!

It transpired that the new pumps were just a little too powerful for the town's old and decrepit pipe-work and simply blew the tops off all the stop-valves, much to the delight of the hundreds of children in the area. For Proni, meanwhile, it was a case of 'back to the drawing board'!

A telephone call from Bob brought me into the A4 office. He and Keith, the regional commander, were studying a large map of Brčko District.

'Hi, Graham; you are just the person we need to talk to. Come and have a look at this,' said Keith, waving a hand over the map.

He expressed his concern that the current patrol areas were set out in such a way that the local police were only policing areas of a single ethnicity. This was only natural, because of the three police stations within the district; one was commanded by a Muslim, one by a Croat and one by a Serb officer, with Chief Kokanovic being senior to all three. Keith's request was simple: I was to talk to the three commanders and get them to agree on new patrol sectors so that each policed all three ethnic communities.

I returned to the office and told Will of the objective.

'Getting three police chiefs to agree on an issue such as this will be like pissing into the wind!' said Will.

I had to agree. The problem was the 'Inter-Entity Boundary Line', which ran right through the middle of Brčko District. The Muslim officers on the Federation side were reluctant to cross over and police Serbian-dominated villages, and the same was true in reverse for the Serbian officers. As for the Croat officers, they had skilfully managed to patrol a corridor that led right up to the Croatian border. This problem was going to take some skilled diplomacy if democratic policing was to succeed in Brčko.

Will arranged a meeting with all three of the chiefs. I meanwhile spoke to Kokanovic and informed him of my intentions, the bonus being that I knew he trusted our judgement and would give us his support.

'So how are we going to play this?' asked Will.

'Reverse psychology. My intention is to present to the chiefs a map giving my idea of the new patrol areas which I know they will not accept; hopefully they will work together to offer a better solution,' I suggested.

'It might just work!' agreed Will.

The following Monday, the meeting was held. Protests came from all directions, but my reply was short and to the point: 'Gentlemen, if you do not agree to my suggestion, then work together and create a solution of your own. However, the UN will not accept any plan that contains ethnic corridors, selective patrolling or use of the IEBL as some kind of border. You have one week to create a new map!'

Will, Dragan and I quickly left the room, and the police chiefs' arguing echoed along the full length of the corridor.

A week later, we again sat in the meeting room. Dragan sat on my left, Kokanovic on my right, and next to him was Will. This time, however, we were to do the listening.

Pinned to the wall was a map of Brčko District upon which had been drawn three defined patrol sectors. Each police chief then spoke for 15 minutes and described the merits of policing the new areas, having taken into

93

consideration such things as manpower, equipment and the geographical layout of the terrain.

My attention was firmly fixed on the map; could it be true or were my eyes deceiving me? I followed the broken line that identified the IEBL along from the west of the country to the east, but where it passed through Brčko District it had been erased!

Will had seen it too. 'I think we have just witnessed an historic moment!' he said.

He was right; democratic policing had indeed come to exist in Bosnia, and Kokanovic congratulated his commanders.

Pero Duric lit a cigarette. 'See, you can achieve anything when you put aside politics!' he said.

The local police now made an extra effort to clean up the town. Up until now, there had been a blind eye turned upon the unlawful practice of prostitution. The 'noc clubs' were filled with women from Eastern Europe, some of whom willingly worked their trade, as they could earn large sums of money compared to the low earnings they achieved back in their home countries. However, there were also a large number of women who had been tricked into coming to Bosnia by being offered high salaries to work as erotic dancers in café bars. Once they were on site, the bar owners would take away the girls' passports and force them to work as prostitutes for three to six months before handing their passports back.

Most of the women came from Ukraine, and, for those who wanted to leave, the easiest way to achieve this was to quietly mention this fact to the police when they raided the club; they would then be technically arrested and given free passage back to their home country.

I was constantly surprised by the fact that, when the police interviewed the women, it was revealed that they were well educated and highly skilled. It was not uncommon to find a prostitute in Brčko who was an architect or a doctor back in her home country.

The trafficking of people was not just restricted to women; there were those who sought to exploit refugees from foreign countries as far away as the Middle East. These parasites of society preyed on those seeking a better life and were quick to take advantage of a country that was trying to recover from war and whose borders were vulnerable and easily bypassed.

On one such occasion a number of Chinese migrants had travelled their way across eastern Russia and through to Croatia. To enter Bosnia they had to cross the River Sava, avoiding the usual border crossing, naturally. The migrants were herded into small rowing boats by their crooked exploiters and set adrift under the cover of darkness.

The Sava may look picturesque, but it has a strong and vicious current, and a boat without power would simply spin out of control and capsize, spilling its human cargo into the water. It was the families living along the edge of the river who alerted the police, having heard the screams of panic as the helpless victims were dragged along by the current.

Only 14 made it to the shore; it was estimated that as many as ten people drowned that night.

CHAPTER 7

DECISIONS

Dragan and I left Brčko and headed off towards Zagreb Airport in Croatia. The purpose of this trip was to meet my daughter Lindsey and brother Peter, who had flown out to spend a short holiday with me. I had not seen Lindsey for nearly a year and was looking forward to our reunion.

'Dad!' she squealed as she threw her arms around me. Although only 15 years old, she certainly did look very much a young woman.

'Hi, bro; thanks for bringing her.'

'No problem, mate; I have been looking forward to this trip.'

We chatted constantly during the drive back to Brčko. Dragan dropped us off at the house and my two guests unpacked.

'*Alo, cao Grem*?' called Stoja as she entered the house.

I took care of the introductions in local language.

'*Tvoj cerka naljepša Grem*!'

'Stoja says you are beautiful, Lindsey.'

'*Hvala*,' she replied to Stoja, having quickly grasped the basic courtesies.

Although it was late into the evening, my guests were far too excited to be tired, so we drove into town and entered the Galaxy bar; Niko and Dragan were already there. Lindsey quickly became the centre of attention; the local girls became fascinated by the length of my daughter's hair, which flowed down the full length of her back. Dragan stayed close beside her and acted as interpreter and personal bodyguard.

Knowing that in his company she was safe, I could then spend time introducing my brother to other friends. Neso, a local Serb, looked very similar in appearance to Peter, so much so that they were often mistaken for brothers. One thing was for sure: they both shared the same sense of humour.

The week passed quickly, but then it always does when you are having a good time.

Lindsey enjoyed her stay and made a lot of new friends. Some of our time was spent going to the local swimming pool at Bijeljina, and this, being a sulphur spring, was heated. We were also invited to a Serbian wedding party; here Lindsey impressed the local youths with her ability to shoot a gun, having been trained in the use of firearms during her stay in America. She wasted no time in dismembering a tree with the aid of a pump-action shotgun.

Our final evening was spent at Stoja's house, where we all enjoyed one of Dusan's familiar barbecues. Rada and Milka gave her gifts to remember her stay in Brčko; in fact, by the time they left they needed an extra suitcase to put them in. Such was the kindness of the local people.

Govinda was coming to the end of his mission and was soon to return to Nepal.

'Good morning, Govinda; how are you?'

'I am well, sir, but sad that I must return to Nepal at the end of the month.'

'Yes, we will miss you; you have done well here.'

After he left the office, I telephoned Bob and suggested that a commendation be given to Govinda. Bob agreed and suggested that Will design a formal-looking certificate to be presented at a later date; meanwhile, Keith would send a letter of commendation to him.

Govinda was filled with joy, for this was the Holy Grail that he had sought; now he would achieve the promotion that he desperately wanted.

Returning from lunch, Will and I entered the office. Govinda was at the computer, typing feverishly. I looked over his shoulder at the monitor screen and laughed.

A worried look fell across Govinda's face. 'My work is not typing good?'

'No, no, it is perfect, but what exactly are you doing?'

'Sir, you are giving me a letter of commendation, but this I must send to my superiors in Nepal, and I will have nothing to hang on my wall!'

'Oh, now I get the idea, but listen: I know we are in the millennium year, but do you not think the title of "United Nations Officer of the Millennium" is going a bit far?'

'Oh my God!' he exclaimed, his head nodding from side to side.

A few days later he was summoned to the regional commander's office, where Keith formally presented him with a certificate of merit. He was so proud and invited me and Bob to his home for an evening dinner, which we were glad to accept.

Govinda met me and Bob at the door and invited us in. At first I thought he was into a bit of cross-dressing, but then I realised he was wearing his national costume, and very smart he looked.

On entering the living room, Bob and I sat on the sofa; Govinda sat on the floor.

'Will you be drinking whisky, sir?'

'Thank you; that would be fine'

He then crawled out of the room, only standing when he had reached the door.

Bob and I looked curiously at each other.

He returned, again on his knees, holding a very fine bottle of whisky and two tall glass tumblers, one of which he filled to the brim!

'Govinda, may I stop you for a moment?'

'You are not liking, sir?'

'Oh, yes, but only in a small glass, please.'

He crawled out of the room again and returned with two small Rakija glasses and a plate of what looked like small spicy chicken legs coated in breadcrumbs. I started to eat these and found them very tasty indeed.

Each time Govinda left the room, he would crawl, never standing.

'Govinda, please relax; we are here as your friends.'

'Oh no, sir, you are my gods; I must never be so rude as to stand above you!'

I was totally humbled; here was a man with such kindness and humility that I felt unworthy to be in his presence. What a shame it was that such manners and courtesy no longer existed in the UK. So arrogant are we in the west that we have the audacity to refer to Nepal as a third-world country.

'Govinda, these taste really nice, but where did you find such small chicken legs?'

'It is not chicken, sir, they are a delicacy from Nepal: spiced pigeon legs!'

'But where do you buy pigeon legs in Brčko?'

Govinda left the room and returned holding a high-powered air rifle. 'I am not buying, sir; I am catching in the garden today, very fresh!'

Bob and I howled with laughter; the thought of a Nepalese sniper in Brčko did nothing to improve his stature.

The end of the month came and Govinda left Brčko to return home.

About a week later, Bob received an e-mail from him and rang me. It transpired that Govinda did get promoted to police commander upon his return to Nepal; however, as soon as his plane touched down at the airport, he was whisked off to a waiting helicopter to spend a year in the jungle fighting terrorists.

Good luck, Govinda, I thought to myself.

Throughout my childhood I was compelled to attend church and as a result resented having to sit and listen to a priest droning on about righteousness and being forgiving. It always seemed to me that those who attended church did so not so much out of a strong Christian belief as because it was the right place for a middle-class family to be seen in and as such treated the church as a fashion accessory.

As an adult I simply chose not to bother with such matters, but here in Brčko I found myself attending church on a regular basis and could not offer a logical reason why. There was no burning bush or holy vision, just a strong desire to spend a few moments alone and contemplate my own existence.

I found that I had begun to question myself and dislike the selfish person that normal living had made me become. Here in Brčko, life was far from perfect and for the local people it was a constant daily struggle just to survive, yet everybody that I met retained their respect and dignity.

For the people of the town, the church gave hope for the future.

Dragan and I sat drinking coffee in the morning sunshine. The white Orthodox church across the road reflected the sun's rays, giving the building an orange glow.

'Dragan, I have decided to change my faith to Orthodox; would you be willing to be my godfather?'

'Yes, of course; it would be a great honour.'

'Thank you, but I would like to keep my decision between us and the church.'

'Yes, I understand; no problem, mate.'

We crossed the street and entered the church, where I was introduced to the priest and Dragan explained my desire to convert. The priest handed me a red leather-bound Bible and asked that I read it first; if I still wished to convert, he would be glad to welcome me to the Orthodox faith.

I was relieved to see that the Bible was in both local and English language, but it was not as I expected. I thought I would be reading phrases such as 'in the beginning there was man' or 'Joshua beget Solomon who beget Moses' etc. Instead, the book explained the reasons and meaning behind the different services and celebrations; I even came to understand the meaning behind St George and the slaying of the dragon.

For the next week, I would sit beside the swimming pool and read, although I did get some very strange looks from people when Beba asked if I would put some sun cream on her back. I suppose it would look strange to see a man holding a Bible in one hand while smearing sun cream onto the back of a very attractive young woman with the other.

When I had read the book, I returned to the church and confirmed my desire to convert. A date was set for the following Wednesday, after morning prayers.

The day came: Wednesday 27 September 2000. I put on my grey suit and walked into town. Dragan was already waiting by the church gate; he looked smart, dressed in black and wearing a tie, the latter being something he rarely did.

We crossed ourselves as we entered the church. Two priests were waiting for us at the altar, and both were dressed in finely decorated robes.

One priest spoke the service in local language, while the other very quietly translated.

The priest crossed my forehead, my wrists and my ankles and then led the way as we all walked in a circle with Dragan behind me, his hands placed upon my shoulders. I was then asked the holy questions and responded to each of these in local language.

I was to be known as 'Nikola' and my appointed saint's day was to be Nikodan, which was on 19 December and celebrated St Nicholas, the patron saint of travellers from over the sea.

It was a simple, private and humble service and confirmed my renewed faith in God.

My time in Brčko had drawn to a close and, as I reflected on the past year, a sense of achievement came over me. We as a team had done many things, and the policies and projects that we had created were now being implemented by other agencies throughout Bosnia.

OSCE now took up the role of training a press officer for each police division within the country. Medica Zenica were training police officers in how to deal with and investigate sensitive issues such as rape and domestic violence. The Bosnian border police had been reformed into a multi-ethnic force, receiving a new identity and insignia, and community police officers were trained and deployed throughout the country to build trust and confidence within the local communities.

The Brčko District pilot scheme had been a huge success for the United Nations and all the international agencies that were and still are actively involved. Brčko had returned to peace and unified living. Yes, of course there was still a long way to go, but the town was leading the way forward.

I could only hope that the rest of the country would be able to catch up with the pace of change that had occurred here.

Bob, Wayne and Keith now boarded the coach that was to take them to Sarajevo for their return flight home. Gill and I were to stay for just a few more days, as she was travelling home by car with friends and I was having new crowns fitted to my teeth by Branka, one of my language assistants, who ran a dental practice in the town centre. Many people wanted to share my time during this final week, and a party was held at the Galaxy so that my friends could say goodbye.

My final evening was spent the same way as my first, enjoying one of Stoja's wonderful barbecue evenings. Milka and Rada gave more gifts for me to pass on to my daughter Lindsey. I did not want to leave and would have willingly stayed, but I knew that I had to go.

Dragan and Niko drove me to Zagreb Airport and we shook hands.

'This is not goodbye; we know that you will come back soon,' said Dragan.

'Thank you both for everything and for making me so welcome in Brčko,' I replied, and then I walked through to the departure gate.

Back in England I now faced a decision: did I resign from the police force and return to Brčko, or did I stay and just be grateful for the experience?

There was still a lot to do in Bosnia. Others could carry on the work and do the job just as well as I could, but here in England anything I did would pale into insignificance compared to the assistance that could be given to the citizens of Bosnia.

As I stood in the rear garden of my brother's home, I watched the flicker of lights from a plane as it traced its way across the starlit sky. My heart yearned to be on board.

'I will return one day.'

'*Samo za tebe slatkis moj.*'

'*Vidimo se.*'

END OF PART ONE

Nikola's Passage

Part Two

'If you feed the birds,
God will feed you'

Orthodox Parable

With love to Lindsey
XXX

And my thanks to
Will, Dragan, Beba, Niko, Jim and all my friends in Brčko

CHAPTERS

PART TWO

CHAPTER 8

REUNION OF FRIENDS

'Caged lions make bad house pets.'

I found myself pacing about the house in a state of frustrated boredom, so I made the decision to return to Bosnia. My length of stay would be determined by one of two factors: first, could I secure a position with another international agency, and, if not, how long would my savings last?

The decision to leave the police force was a huge gamble and, from a personal viewpoint, I hated gambling, as I would always lose. But the opportunity to continue working in Bosnia was too good to miss, and an unconfirmed appointment with an American agency called ICITAP was just the kind of position that I was looking for.

All that I required was a 'yes' vote from the US state department to confirm the position, so it made sense to return and wait in Brčko.

Dragan was waiting for me in the arrivals hall; his beaming smile said that he was pleased to see me again, and we shook hands.

'Hello, mate, welcome back; a lot of people have missed you.'

'It is good to see you. How are things back in Brčko?'

'*Svaki dan isto stranja!*'

I quickly ran the translation through my head: *every day, the same shit*. There were one or two people back in England who would want to use that phrase, I thought.

I tossed my bags into the rear of his car and climbed into the passenger seat.

Dragan lit two cigarettes and handed one to me, after which he drove like a demon out of Zagreb, taking great delight in cutting up the other road users, who were Croatian, naturally. 'They will see the Bosnian plates on this car and swear and curse at me,' he said, glancing into his rear-view mirror.

'Do you not think that the Croatian police may want to give you a ticket?'

Dragan pulled out the UN identity card that hung from a chain around his neck. 'UN diplomatic immunity!' he said, laughing, and accelerated hard along the fast lane of the dual carriageway.

To a certain degree he was right; the showing of the UN identity card to any local police officer would see you on your way without any delay or harassment.

We crossed the border into Bosnia. Dragan opened the glove box and took out two bottles of local Nik beer. These he opened very skilfully using one hand and a disposable lighter, then, passing a bottle to me, he said, '*Zivili!*'

'*Zivili kume,*' I responded, remembering to look into his eyes.

Dragan just smiled.

As we drove along the road to Lončari junction, I could see the now familiar mine warning tape that snaked its way along both sides of the road, and as we passed the large blue sign that announced that we had entered Brčko District a sense of homecoming came over me. I was glad to be back.

Brčko had changed little, the most notable difference being the addition of new floors to the blocks of flats that filled the town centre. The local people were still filling plastic bottles with drinking water from the tap that was never turned off and traffic still threw up clouds of dust that choked the lungs each time you breathed, but this was where I wanted to be.

Dragan pulled into a parking space outside the Galaxy bar. 'Let's go, mate; you have friends waiting to see you,' and he led the way inside.

'*Cao Gavro, cao Nikola, kako si Gavro?*' calls came from every direction. I responded to each by shaking hands and kissing each person on the cheeks three times, which is the traditional way to greet a Serb. Damir was a Croatian-Serb and being christened a Catholic; I respectfully kissed him only twice.

'*Jesi kume!*' came a shout that I instantly recognised.

'*Cao Niko, kako si danas?*'

Niko's reply was to give me a bear hug that stretched the spinal cord to its limits.

As I stood beside the bar, people approached asking me questions about life in England. They found it hard to comprehend when I told them that they had a better lifestyle in Brčko, despite the fact that they lack the material luxuries that we westerners take for granted.

I did not want to offend my friends, but I was keen to see Stoja, just to let her know that I had arrived and have a coffee. I told my friends that I would return shortly and left the bar to walk down to the port where she worked as a cashier for a local bank. Excitement caused my pace to quicken.

Having reached the single-storey building, situated alongside the Sava River, I entered the office. Stoja was sat talking to a female colleague, who left upon seeing me.

Stoja kept her composure until her colleague had departed, then, upon closing the door, she threw her arms around me and kissed me softly on the cheek. '*Kako si Grem?*'

'*Ja sam sretan sad.*'

109

Stoja smiled. '*Isto ja,*' she replied.

She left the office and quickly returned with two cups of coffee and a small pile of sugar lumps; these she would dip into her coffee and gently nibble, giving me a coy smile as she did so.

We sat and talked, and she explained that, as new monitors were living in her brother's home, she was unable to give me a room to stay in. I put her mind at ease by telling her that Beba and Dragan had arranged a new flat for me in the centre of town.

Her mouth broke into a smile. '*Ti si moj slatkis, znac,*' she said.

Being called one's sweetness was a kind term of endearment, I thought.

I finished my coffee and told Stoja that I would see her soon; she discreetly kissed me again, and I returned to the Galaxy.

Dragan was standing beside the bar and, on seeing me, handed me a paper tissue.

'What's this for?'

'Wipe your face!'

I took the tissue and wiped my face. I could clearly see the dark red stain that now coated it. 'Oops!'

Dragan just smiled and said nothing.

A short while later, Beba joined us. 'Have you seen your new flat yet?' she asked.

'No, we were waiting for you,' I replied.

'You will like the street name.'

'Why?'

'It is called Nikola Pasic!'

I ran the English equivalent through my mind. 'Nikola's Passage: how amazing; that would make an excellent title for a good book!'

We left the bar and went to view the flat.

The property was located on the third floor of a long apartment block, and upon reaching the entrance door we were met by a Muslim couple who owned the flat. After the usual introductions they invited us inside.

The flat comprised two main rooms. On my right was a kitchen diner, which had a door that led out onto a veranda and offered excellent views across the town. To my left was the living room, which also served as the bedroom, having a king-size sofa bed; this room also had a door that led to another veranda. Between the two rooms were the toilet and bathroom.

The flat was perfect; it was clean, well-furnished and had satellite TV, and, at 300 marks per month, it was very good value.

I paid my first month's rent and my landlord left me to get settled in. Dragan and Beba helped me unpack, and after a quick cup of coffee they too left.

I had planned to spend my first night alone in my new home and settled down to watch television; this, however, was not to be the case. About 9.30pm my solitude was disturbed by a knock at the door.

I got up off the sofa bed and opened the front door. In marched a line of bodies, each clutching bottles of beer and wine; some carried boxes of pizza.

'*Cao*, Nikola; house party!' said Sladjana as she kissed me on the cheek.

I could do no more than watch by the door as the conga line of bodies spread out into my new apartment, and with twenty or so guests my little flat did look crowded!

Niko opened a bottle of beer and thrust it into my hand. '*Zivili kume!*' he said, before disappearing into the throng of bodies to grab a slice of pizza.

Milan loaded a CD into the stereo, and out blasted very lively folk music.

'Oh, what the heck? OOPAH!' I shouted, joining the group of women who were dancing in a ring with Dragan in the middle.

This was indeed a very pleasant welcome back.

The party went on till the early hours, but my guests were not only kind; they were considerate as well. When it was time to leave, all of them worked together to clean up and dispose of the empty bottles and cans; they even did the washing up!

The following morning I was feeling rather delicate; the bright sunshine hurt my eyes and the constant throbbing in my head was painful. Oh, yes, this was a hangover, and my stomach wasted no time in rejecting the cup of coffee that I had made for myself.

I showered, dressed and walked into town; the fresh air quickly cleared my headache, so I chose to sit outside a café bar and have a fruit juice as I watched the bustle of daily life pass by.

It is true when people say that if you stand still long enough you will meet again every person you ever knew, for now, as I sat, everyone I knew in Brčko passed by and stopped to say hello.

'*Jo jesi kume*?' a familiar voice called from the end of the street. Niko approached, holding his arms up in the air. 'Where are you? I have looked everywhere for you!'

'I have been here all morning getting rid of this hangover!'

'Yes, OK, but today I saw Stoja; she tells me to ask you to go to her home for a barbecue tonight. Will you go?'

'Do pigs fly?'

'*Molim*?' Niko frowned, not understanding my rhetorical statement.

'Yes, of course I will.'

By now the waiter had joined us, and, after politely waiting for our conversation to end, he asked, '*Dobro utro, izvolite?*'

Niko thought for a moment, then turned to me. 'Will you have a beer with me?'

'Niko, after last night I don't think my stomach would appreciate any more alcohol'

'*Stranja*! Beer now is good, how you say, dog hair!'

'I think you mean the hair of the dog. Go on, then, just one.'

Niko turned to the waiter. '*Dva pivo i dva rakija molim.*'

'For God's sake, Niko, my stomach will not thank you for this!'

We sat and talked for the next hour, during which he explained to me that Will was back in America on holiday but would be returning to Brčko in four days' time. I was glad of this, as I looked forward to seeing Will again.

Just then, as if by magic, Will appeared in front of us.

'Hi, Will; I thought you were in the States.'

'Well, hi, my friend; I knew there was a reason why I had to come back early!'

'So how is Babs?'

'Great; we have just bought some land with a small ranch house near to my home in Texas, so now I have to work like a slave to pay for it!'

Will declined the offer of a beer on the grounds that it was only midday, then turned to the waiter and said, 'I will have pear brandy with pear juice, *molim*.'

Niko and I both laughed, but then Will never did anything by halves.

'So have you heard anything from ICITAP?'

'No, not yet; I am just going to have to wait for a reply from the US state department.'

'Don't worry; I know everyone is pushing for you.'

I finished my drink and left my friends in order to go shopping for food and get ready for Stoja's barbecue. It had been Stoja's birthday on 1 October, but I had missed this as I was back in England; however, I did have a small gift for her and I knew she would like what I had to give.

When I arrived at the house around 6.00pm, Rada saw me approaching and came bouncing down the driveway.

'Hello, Grem, are you fine?' She broke into fits of giggles.

'Yes, I am very fine; are you fine?'

'Yes, I am still very fine, thank you; did you miss me so much that you had to return?

'Oh, most definitely!'

She gave me a welcoming hug, then took my hand and led me to the rear garden. '*Cao mama, imam Grem!*'

Stoja was busy preparing a salad, while Dusan, his face obscured by the smoke from the barbecue, cooked pork steaks. He stabbed at the meat with a long-handled fork and offered a piece to me.

'DUSAN!' scolded Stoja.

Dusan returned the meat to the barbecue and offered another piece, this time on a plate.

Milka then pulled into the driveway and shrieked to a halt in my old Bosna-car. I had given her the vehicle as a gift prior to my leaving Brčko and the car was now her pride and joy. She and her fiancé now joined the rest of us. '*Cao Grem, kako si*?'

'*Dobro hvala*; how is the car running?'

'Just super, but you cannot have it back!'

'Don't worry; it is yours forever.'

Stoja had already pre-cooked some food in the house, and this she now brought out on large silver platters and bowls. She was a good cook and served a meal of chicken coated in breadcrumbs, salad, boiled potatoes and 'sarma', a traditional dish of rolled cabbage leaves stuffed with rice and small pieces of meat and boiled in a vegetable stock. These were particularly delicious and very filling. As usual, the meal was washed down with copious amounts of red wine.

After the meal we sat in the garden and chatted. The girls, Milka and Rada, retired upstairs to study for their degrees, happy in the knowledge that my local language skills were of such a standard that I could chat without the aid of an interpreter.

Stoja said that she was sad that I had not been in Brčko for her birthday, and the mention of this reminded me that I had a gift for her hidden in my jacket, which now lay in the hall. I quickly fetched the gift, the offer of which surprised her. She giggled with anticipation.

I placed the gift into her hands and she hurriedly tore open the wrapping.

'*Mobili telefon za mene! Hvala lijepo Grem.*' She threw her arms around me and kissed me repeatedly on the neck, then dashed upstairs to show the girls her new toy. A mobile telephone was the number one must-have luxury in Brčko!

Around midnight Dusan gave me a lift home. Nikola Pasic, the street where I lived, was unusually busy, with smartly-dressed people walking along in alcohol-induced happiness. They had obviously been to a wedding party, as the men still had flowers in their jacket lapels. Love conquers all, even depression, I thought to myself as I climbed the stairs to my apartment.

Once inside, I slid under my duvet and, with a smile upon my face, I drifted off to sleep.

It was the sound of the church bells that woke me up with a start the following morning.

'Blast, I am late!'

Having quickly shaved and dressed, I walked into town. The sun shone brightly, but there was a definite chill in the air and I knew that winter was fast approaching.

Niko screeched his car to a halt and waved to me from the other side of the street. In a typical local manner, he did a U-turn in the road, causing a plethora of angry car horns as he obstructed the oncoming traffic, then abandoned his car half on and half off the pavement. '*Cao kume, dobro utro, sta radis?*'

'Good morning, Niko; I was going to church, but I think I am too late.'

A passing motorist honked his car horn and Niko responded by making a rude gesture with his hand, then exclaimed, 'Oh, shit, that is my uncle!'

'I do not think he will be too pleased with the way you say good morning to him!'

Niko just shrugged his shoulders. 'I am thinking that you have missed church; look!' He pointed to the line of people now coming out of the tall white Orthodox building.

'Oh, well, I will go later.'

'If you are not busy, would you like to come to my village? Mercy Corps are going to rebuild my father's house, but first we must clear the base of building stones.'

'I think you mean building rubble.'

'Some of that, too! But I do have beer and food.'

'OK, then, let's go.'

We drove out of Brčko District and down an unmade winding road until we came to Vitanovic; this was Niko's village, and before the war Serbs and Croats had lived together peacefully as friends there. He pointed out each house and told me the ethnicity of the occupants; it seemed to me to be a 50/50 mix of Serb and Croat.

'This was my grandfather's farm,' he said, as we drove past a destroyed house with outbuildings that would have housed pigs or cows.

'Here is my uncle's home,' he continued, as we approached a large pile of broken bricks and concrete, which sat next to the farm.

'And here is our home; well, it will be when it has been rebuilt!'

I viewed the scene of total destruction and felt very sorry for Niko and his family. What was ironic was the fact that neither Muslims nor Croats had caused this destruction; it had been done by the Serbian army while passing through on its way to Srebrenica, and Niko and his family were themselves Serbs!

I also noticed that all of the Croat homes were already rebuilt and occupied; in fact, judging by the manicured gardens, they had been rebuilt some time ago. I asked Niko why none of the Serbian homes had been rebuilt.

'They are Croats; the international people built their homes first, and we are Serbs and were blamed for the war, so we must wait longer.' There was sadness and resignation in his voice.

No one disputed the fact that Milošević was responsible for the war, not even the Serbian residents of Brčko, but I still felt that this policy of preferred donor aid was slightly biased and unfair. I would raise this point with Ambassador Matthews the next time we spoke.

The task in hand was simple enough; all we had to do was pick up the rubble and toss it into what used to be the rear garden. We had cleared a large area when Niko walked over to his car and produce two bottles of beer and a large pork sandwich that had been cut into two halves. He handed me a bottle of beer and one half of the sandwich.

'*Zivili*,' I said.

'*Zivili kume*,' he replied, stuffing the sandwich into his mouth with a grubby hand covered in cement dust.

'I don't suppose you have any water yet?'

'Mmmmm, yes, come.'

He led me to the corner of the front garden; there lay a metal plate surrounded by a low brick wall. Lifting the plate revealed a very deep water well.

Niko drank directly from the tap that was attached to the brick wall. 'See, we have good clean water, not like that shitty stuff in town.'

Fearing that my body did not have all the antibodies that a local would have, I politely declined to drink it.

We continued clearing the rubble, and then Niko drove me back to Brčko.

'When the house is rebuilt, you must come for a barbecue and meet the rest of my relatives and neighbours.'

'Yes, I would like that very much, Niko; thank you.'

There, in the town centre, we sat outside a café bar and bathed in the afternoon sunshine. It was such a relaxing and pleasant end to a day of hard work.

CHAPTER 9

NIKODAN

A few days had passed, and I had now got into the routine of meeting Will and the rest of the team for morning coffee at the 'San Marino' café bar next to the police station; this was affectionately referred to as the 'outside office'. I was no longer a UN monitor, but as a volunteer I was able to assist in any projects that were being undertaken, and as such I was able to stay in the loop and keep informed of what was going on behind the scenes.

A major problem was growing concerning the local college students and the newly formed multi-ethnic schools. The students were protesting at being taught by teachers of mixed ethnicity, and Muslim students who were leaving anti-Serbian graffiti on the walls and desks aggravated this.

'Graham, why not have an informal chat with the education minister? She trusts you and may be grateful for any ideas you have that may offer a solution to her problems,' suggested Will.

'OK, I will see if she would like to have lunch'

Unfortunately, lunch had to wait, for the next day the students held a demonstration in the town centre during which a number of UN vehicles were vandalised.

A few days after the incident, the education minister Mariana Mladic and I met up for coffee at the bakery.

'Grem, a solution must be found; this situation is making the curriculum unworkable.'

'Would it be possible to have a broader gap between the ethnic groups and have one group attend an evening class? This way the students would not clash.'

'That may be a solution. I have a meeting with Mayor Kisic tomorrow to discuss the problem; maybe I will suggest this.' She paid for the coffee and then left.

A few days later, the schools did adopt an evening class and peace and harmony returned, for now at least.

19 December was Nikodan, St Nicholas's day, and, as a newly christened member of the Orthodox faith, this was the day I celebrated my appointed saint.

It being my first saint day, I quite naturally wanted to follow all of the traditional customs. My friends were very willing to assist me; this was a special time for them as well, as they were to bear witness to the very first Englishman to celebrate an Orthodox saint day in Brčko.

Stoja gave me a short but wide glass filled with dried sweetcorn; this I was to take to the church to be blessed, after which I would return the corn to Stoja. She was to soak the corn with honey overnight, and this would form the blessed offering with which to start my saint day meal.

I was already aware that my celebration meal could not contain animal fat or meat, but fish was the accepted traditional dish. Now I needed to seek advice on what sort of fish and how much. I again turned to Stoja, explaining to her that I intended to have 15 guests at the table.

'*Super, treba ti jedan saran i petnaest pastrumka!*'

Good, one carp and 15 trout; that should not be too difficult to obtain, I thought.

She told me that the carp would be used to make a fish soup called '*pasud*' and that the trout should be stuffed and baked in foil; this would serve as the main course. Stoja would make the soup for me.

Dusan arrived early at the flat and beeped the horn of his car to announce his arrival; this was good, as the best fish was had first thing in the morning.

We drove to the fishmonger and I went inside, leaving Dusan to wait in the car. A large man stood behind the wooden butcher's block, wearing a white apron that was heavily stained with fish blood. In between gutting and filleting fish, he sprinkled sawdust on the floor to soak up the mess.

'*Dobro utro izvolite?*' he said.

'*Dobro utro, ja hoce jedan saran molim.*'

'*Moze, veliki u marli?*'

This question I gave some thought: large or small? As I had 15 guests attending this meal, I decided to go for a large one. '*Veliki molim!*'

The fishmonger now gestured for me to join him beside a very large water tank, and it was now that I realised that the buying of fish was not quite the same as in England, for now I was looking into a tank of live fish!

He dipped a large net into the tank and lifted out a carp, the like of which I had never seen before. It was enormous, at least 18 inches from its dorsal fin to the base of a fat round belly. He stuffed the now thrashing fish into a plastic carrier bag and handed it to me.

'*Kraj zivot molim?*' I asked.

The fishmonger took the bag containing the fish and gave it a hefty 'thwack' with a wooden rolling pin. As he passed the bag back to me, the fish burst into life again. I handed back the bag, and he laid this on the block and repeatedly struck the fish.

'*Zivot kraj, sigurno!*' he exclaimed, confirming the fish as deceased.

I passed the bag to Dusan, then returned to the shop and ordered 15 trout; these the man caught and despatched without any problem.

After paying a mere 30 marks for the fish, Dusan and I returned to Stoja, and upon arrival I proudly presented the fish to her.

She looked into the bag containing the large carp and frowned, then she quickly went into the kitchen and returned holding a large saucepan that was now dwarfed by the fish. Stoja looked at the pan, then the fish, and then she looked at me. '*Grem, kako ja radim molim*?'

Milka and Rada now walked into the room. They too looked at the pan and the fish, then they looked at their mother and burst into laughter.

Stoja just stood with folded arms, her tongue in her cheek, and smiled.

'Grem, are you intending to feed the whole of Brčko with that fish?' asked Milka.

'Are you suggesting that my fish is a bit on the large side?'

'Large, no, of course not, but I think my mother would like to know how you expect her to get this fish into this pan!' Milka waved the pan and fish at me in a mocking fashion.

'I see; well, I am feeding 15 people.'

'Only 15! Grem, this fish will make enough *pasud* to feed fifty!'

My fish was obviously too big, and I apologised to Stoja.

'You are crazy Englishman!' she said, pressing the cheeks of my face together with both hands, and then she smiled.

A larger pan was obtained from the garage, and Stoja went to work creating the dish called *pasud*. Basically, this dish was composed of fish pieces, kidney beans, butter beans, potatoes that were boiled into a soup-like state and, finally, a vegetable stock with added herbs. This was to form the first course of my meal and, as I was to later learn, gave rise to a severe bout of flatulence!

The second course would be stuffed trout, the stuffing being made up of rice, breadcrumbs, sage and lemon zest. This was accompanied with boiled potatoes, shredded cabbage soaked in lemon juice, pickled sweet peppers and 'Ivar', a tomato and garlic sauce that was served cold as a dressing.

Naturally, the whole meal would be washed down with lashings of red wine and Rakija.

My role in the preparation was to gut the trout and carefully remove the spine while leaving the head and tail intact, a job that had a certain amount of risk of personal injury. While I was doing this, Stoja was peeling potatoes.

We were alone in the house, preparing a meal just like a married couple; it felt so right.

Then, as expected, my knife flicked out of the tail end of the fish and stabbed into my left hand.

The wound was small but deep, and Stoja wasted no time in fetching a plaster. We sat close on the sofa; the sweet smell of her perfume was intoxicating. She cleaned the cut and applied the dressing, and then she kissed my hand.

It was the burning smell of overflowing fish soup that caused a mercy dash to the kitchen. Cooking was quickly restored to normal, and I was under strict instruction to guard the soup while Stoja went to the bathroom.

When she returned, she gave me a hug and with her free hand she stirred the soup. I am always impressed by the fact that women are able to concentrate completely on two things at the same time, but then I suppose that is just a woman thing that we mere menfolk were not gifted with!

With the cooking under control, I went into town to buy other essential items. One of these was my 'Hristo hleb' or holy bread. This round loaf was beautiful, having a very ornate religious decoration on the surface; it had been made using flour that had been blessed by the church. Along with the bread, I also purchased a quantity of 'Hristo Kolac';

these small decorative cakes were only produced for saint days and did not contain any animal fat.

The food was prepared, the table set, and my candle was lit as it hung in front of a framed picture of Saint Nikola. The apartment smelt of incense that burned in a small pot; I had wafted this into each corner of the room as a blessing to the apartment.

All was made ready, and I sat anxiously waiting for my guests to arrive. I need not have worried, for precisely at 7.00pm all of my guests arrived and took their places at the table.

I took the bowl of corn that had been soaked in honey, crossed myself and ate a spoonful, and then I passed the bowl to the guest on my right, who stood up and did the same. The bowl continued around the table in this fashion.

Dragan stood up, holding the loaf of bread in both hands; on this Beba had placed a small glass of Rakija spirit. He then spoke a prayer and rotated the loaf of bread, pausing at each rotation to drip three small drops of Rakija spirit onto the loaf. Then he placed the loaf across his left forearm and with his right forearm broke the loaf in half, but not completely. He then turned the loaf again and broke it into quarters before handing the loaf to me.

I placed one quarter onto the shelf beside me and the second quarter I took for myself. The remainder of the loaf I handed to Beba to share amongst the others.

'Oopah!' cried Niko.

Everyone now helped himself or herself to the food while I passed numerous bottles of wine across the table.

'Thank you for doing that, Dragan; I would have had great difficulty trying to say that prayer.'

'No problem, mate; this is your first saint day, so enjoy it!'

I was so pleased that Damir and Toma, who were both Croatian, had accepted my invitation to attend the celebration and took part. More pleasing was the fact that not one of my Serbian guests objected or commented on the fact of their presence; any ethnic differences had been well and truly put aside.

After the meal we retired to the living room, and there we partied on till the early morning hours. When the last of my guests had left, I surveyed the devastation in the kitchen and decided to leave the mess until the following morning.

When I awoke, I quickly realised the mistake I had made in not clearing up before I had gone to bed, for now the apartment stank of stale fish. I opened both patio doors, lit a small incense block and set about the task of cleaning the whole apartment; this was to take me all morning to accomplish.

During the afternoon, I gathered together all the pots and pans that Stoja had lent me and walked to her home to return them.

'*Cao Grem, kako si danas?*'

'*Dobro sam hvala.*'

I thanked Stoja for all her help, and she ushered me inside to have coffee. Soon Dusan, Milka and Rada joined us and I spent the afternoon chatting about my saint day celebration; everyone laughed when I explained the overnight flatulence problem I had had whilst buried under my duvet.

CHAPTER 10

STRANGE TIMES

Considering it was late December, it was unusually mild; the sun shone and it was still warm enough to walk about in a pullover.

Dragan had an urge to go fishing by a lake that was situated on the far side of Lončari junction and asked me if I would like to join him and Niko. I accepted the offer and met the pair in the Galaxy; the trip had now become an excuse to have a barbecue, and several others had decided to join us.

At the lakeside, rods were baited and left unattended in the water. Niko had lit his homemade barbecue, and on this he was cooking small sausage-shaped meatballs called *cevapi*. I was most impressed by his engineering skills when I noticed that his barbecue was in fact made out of an old steel disc cutter taken from a farmer's plough. The rotisserie, which now turned pieces of chicken, had started life as a wiper motor from old VW car, presumably powered by the same car's old battery!

The rest of us went to explore a large floating raft that was in the process of construction. It was made up of hundreds of steel bars that had been welded together to form a frame and then supported on several large oil drums which floated the entire platform. A tarpaulin had been stretched across the whole thing to form a roof. We were to learn that this floating pontoon was being built to hold a wedding reception early in the new year, but for now we chose to use it as a place for an impromptu game of cricket. The game soon descended into an amusing farce and only ceased when Niko called us over to eat.

We sat in the afternoon sunshine and talked, but I sensed that all was not well with Niko; outwardly he appeared fine, but something was on his mind. 'Does something worry you, Niko?'

'I have big problem at work and must see the Chief of Crime Police tomorrow.' There was a tone of embarrassment in his voice, and so I suggested that we go for a walk around the lake where we could talk in private.

As we strolled along the water's edge, Niko explained his problem to me. Following an investigation by the United Nations Internal Affairs unit, it had been discovered that some officers in police forces throughout Bosnia had secured their positions by fraudulent means, in that they had not completed a formal education and had not attended any police training colleges. As a result, the UN had initiated a complete vetting of all police officers in Bosnia, during which it was well publicised that three officers had been convicted of fraud and sent to prison for a period of detention.

For my two local police friends, Niko and Toma, this was to be a cause of great concern. In Toma's case, he was a Croat and had been educated in Dubrovnik; he had received his formal police training at a police college in Croatia. Proving his completed education meant a two-day trip to his old school in Dubrovnik and obtaining certified copies of documents relating to his education.

In Niko's case, however, things were not so straightforward; he had completed his formal police training at a police training college in Banja Luka, but his education was completed at a school just outside the district, and this was now just a pile of rubble with all the documents contained therein being destroyed.

'I do not want to go to prison, but how can I prove I went to school?'

I now understood the gravity of the problem, but I was no longer in the UN and was not in a position to help my friend, who I knew to be an honest, hardworking police officer and who was now very frightened of what the future might bring.

'Don't worry, Niko; we will find a way to resolve this problem.'

We rejoined to the group and did not mention the matter again that day. I knew that I needed to talk to Will.

The following morning, I met Will as usual for morning coffee.

'Good morning, Graham. I am going to see the ambassador this morning; why don't you come along? I know he would be pleased to see you now that you're back.'

'Yes, that would be great, but listen: I need to discuss a problem that Niko is having at work regarding the vetting by internal affairs.' I then related to Will what Niko had told me the previous day.

'He must not try to deal with this problem on his own; the local police are just looking for scapegoats to prove that they are complying with the UN directives. He must get a lawyer to represent his case'

'I agree, Will, but you and I both know that he does not have the means to fund a lawyer; his salary supports his entire family!'

Will thought for a moment. 'Leave this to me. Now drink up; we don't want to keep Ambassador Matthews waiting.'

A few days later Niko was summoned again by the chief of crime police; he was not charged with fraud but was compelled to resign from the police force and would still have to attend a court to answer questions from a judge.

Will and I waited for him to join us at the café bar next door to the police station. When he did, tears filled his eyes; he felt his world was collapsing around him.

He gathered his composure and explained the outcome of the meeting with the crime chief.

Will now went into action. 'Do you have a court date yet, Niko?'

'Not yet, but I am told it will be during February.'

'Good, then we have plenty of time; now I want you to come with me.'

Will and Niko then walked into town.

About an hour had passed and I was about to leave the café bar when Will, Niko and a burly-looking man walked past to enter the police station, I became curious as to what was happening, so I ordered another coffee and waited.

A short while later, Will returned alone and sat down.

'So what is going on?' I asked.

'Niko and his lawyer are talking to the chief of crime police.'

'But he cannot afford a lawyer.'

'Let us just say that money is not an issue.' Will smiled that knowing smile and ordered a coffee.

We did not have to wait long for Niko to join us; when he did, he looked far happier.

'So tell us what happened?'

'My lawyer tells me that I will not go to prison or have a crime record, but as I cannot prove my education I will still have to leave the police force and return some of my salary.' Niko's sense of relief was obvious for all to see.

Will then spoke. 'I have also spoken to the ambassador, and he suggests that you apply for the position of security officer at the new Office of the High Representative building.'

Niko looked stunned. 'You are saying that I have a new job at OHR?'

'Well, not quite; first you must pass the interview and English test.'

Doubt now fell across the face of Niko. 'But my English is not good like Dragan.'

'Trust me, Niko, your English is very good'

Will and I then went into PR mode to prepare him for the interview.

'He will need a new suit,' I said.

'Yes, black, definitely black,' replied Will.

'And a shirt.'

'Yes, white with a dark blue tie.'

I nodded in agreement, then both of us looked at Niko. 'And a full length coat,' I continued.

'Dead right: black, made of wool, nothing cheap, and a black pair of polished shoes.'

'Most definitely: the full executive look!'

'Come on, Niko, you must come with us,' demanded Will.

Niko, now in a state of complete confusion, obeyed without question as we marched him off to a quality tailor's in the town centre.

We entered the shop and presented Niko to the tailor, who scurried about, taking a selection of clothes from the rack and filling Niko's arms.

'Go and try them on,' said Will.

Meanwhile, I selected a full-length woollen overcoat; they looked perfect, and so I chose one for myself as well.

Niko now appeared from the changing room; the transformation from jeans and pullover to a high-class corporate executive was amazing.

'So what do you think, Niko?' asked Will.

'It is great, but I cannot afford these fine clothes.'

'So what do you reckon, Graham: 50/50?' asked Will.

'Sounds fair to me'

We both took out our wallets and settled the bill. Niko was visibly moved by this gesture and thanked us.

Later that week, Niko attended his interview at OHR. Will, Dragan and I waited at the Galaxy bar for him to return.

Niko entered with a smile that stretched from one ear to the other.

'So are we to assume that you got the job, then?' asked Will.

'Yes, and I am getting a salary higher than my dreams. I thank you both with all my soul; you are such good and kind friends.'

The cold weather descended rapidly, overnight in fact, and when I awoke I looked out across the town to see a blanket of snow had fallen, turning the scenery into a picture postcard. The air was fresh and clean, and from the balcony I watched as children played, throwing snowballs at each other. Their laughter filled the street. Christmas had well and truly arrived.

Now, I have to admit I am a practical, common-sense type of person and not one prone to believing in such things as astrology, but today a very strange thing was to occur.

During the summer of 1996, I had dated a woman by the name of Valerie: a lovely woman who in appearance reminded me of the violinist from the Corrs. Valerie would describe our relationship as two ships that tried to pass in the night but kept colliding, and, although we broke up, we remain friends.

Sitting in my apartment, I was surprised when the postman dropped a large envelope through my door. I opened the letter and read the note inside.

Dear Graham,
I was clearing out the cupboard and found your Christmas present that I had intended to give you in 1996, so I thought you might like to have it now, as it is very interesting.

Love Val.

The gift was a booklet: a personal astrological reading done by Jonathan Cainer, giving a forecast for the years to come. What was interesting was the fact that I was about to enter the year of 2001 and so was reading the booklet retrospectively, in the privileged position of being able to compare the information printed against true events that had occurred in my life since 1996.

The booklet made fascinating reading, but what surprised me at this particular moment in time was the fact the Mr Cainer had put into print the words *'The places of interest that you will visit will be Bosnia Yugoslavia.'*

I was speechless; here I was standing in my little apartment in Brčko, Bosnia, reading a document that had been written four years earlier and correctly forecast my visit to this country!

There were many passages that were correct and true, even one that made reference to my mother and stated that she would be an important part of my life. For over twenty years, I had little contact with her; now she and I speak daily and today she is a most important part of my life, as predicted.

I am impressed with Jonathan Cainer's abilities but wonder if it is better not to know what the future holds; then again, six accurately forecasted numbers would be handy!

My very best regards to Mr Cainer.

The party season now went into full swing; each contingent of the IPTF held a party at some point of the festivities. This was a good way of meeting your international colleagues and offered the chance to see how different countries celebrated the Christmas season. But everyone would end up at the Galaxy at some point, so it was here that I chose to spend Christmas.

Police Chief Kokanovic appeared regularly on television to ask the citizens of Brčko not to celebrate the festive season by discharging firearms from the balconies of their homes; the UN and SFOR had obviously prompted this request.

Would the people of Brčko listen and comply? The answer was a definite 'no!' for, at the stroke of midnight, the skies erupted to the sound of gunfire as beads of red tracer bullets snaked across the clear night sky.

Not that this entire display of ordinance was being delivered by the Serbs; the Muslims were also celebrating, as it was the end of Ramadan and the period of fasting was over. Their music and singing could be heard right across town from bars and restaurants.

But amid all this happiness and celebration were moments of abject sadness; as Dragan would say, this was the silly season.

Such a moment had occurred during the night; an elderly woman, depressed with the present and not being able to see a brighter future, chose to end it all by wandering into a minefield.

Despite the pleas from the officers of the IPTF and the local police, who were standing at the edge of the field, the woman ignored their presence and continued to shuffle along in ever-decreasing circles. The officers felt helpless; they could not enter the minefield for fear of risking their own lives and, although they repeatedly begged the woman to stand still, she simply refused to listen.

I was told that it was a quick death, a muffled bang as she fell to the floor amongst the tall grass and gorse bushes. Sadly, she was to remain where she fell for over a week before the army was able to recover her frail and destroyed body.

When will this madness end?

New Year's Eve followed the same routine as that of the year before; as usual, the Galaxy was the venue that all the internationals chose to celebrate the occasion. It was also the place where all the local girls went: to practice their English, of course!

The bar was packed with people, all dressed up for the occasion and looking very attractive indeed. Loud pop music blasted through the speakers and the room was filled with cigarette smoke, which hung like a fog in the air that parted as somebody walked by, only to close in again behind them.

Tonight I sat in a booth with Will, Dragan, Niko, Milan, Sladjana, Neso, Sonja, Damir and Yvette, who was now dating Toma, the Croat policeman. It was a tight squeeze, but nobody objected, as it merely added to the atmosphere. When this got too uncomfortable, Sonja and Sladjana climbed onto the table so that they could dance; the rest of us simply gave a sigh of relief and stretched out in the now vacated spaces.

Dragan tried to talk to me from across the table, but all I could do was laugh as a pair of naked legs danceed from side to side only inches away from my face.

Then two SFOR officers walked into the bar; both were in full military battle fatigues and flak jackets. Upon their thighs hung pistols that were holstered in such a fashion they more suited Wyatt Earp out on a Texas range.

They had not intended to be intimidating, and, being so far away from home, they desperately wanted to share in the fun of this festive night. But the local people had dressed up for this evening, they wanted to party and not be reminded of the horrors of the past and so they ignored the two men.

I looked out of the window; there, parked in a neat row, were the green and black Humvees with cold and wet-looking soldiers standing out of their roofs. It was a shame that they worked while others partied.

Will went over to the two officers and spoke quietly to them. The men marched smartly out of the bar and came to a halt beside the vehicles, where they handed their guns to other soldiers. With a smart about turn, they re-entered the bar.

The girls, wishing to thank them for their consideration, instantly mobbed them with hugs and kisses.

'So tell me, just what was it you said to them, Will?'

'I simply said, "if you want to get laid tonight, leave the guns in the Humvees"!'

'Can anybody lend me a pistol for an hour?'

'Yes, I can!'

'And me!'

'Over here, borrow mine!'

'Jesus Christ, I was only joking!'

The officers declined the offer of a beer, choosing instead to drink cola. After a short while they returned to the vehicles, where the junior soldiers handed over their high-powered rifles and then also entered the bar. Again the local women mobbed them with hugs and kisses. It was good to see the local people treat them as friends; it was, after all, New Year's Eve for the soldiers as well.

As the midnight hour approached we all counted down the seconds.

'Sretna Nova Godina!'

A volley of corks from bottles of sparkling wine shot across the bar and everybody kissed and hugged the person next to them; meanwhile, outside, projectiles of a different kind were being let loose as tracer bullets fired from AK-47's began to snake their way across the clear night sky. Through the town centre drove overexcited youths, who discharged pistols into the air as they hung precariously from the windows of their vehicles.

Back inside the bar, each and every table supported women who danced to loud folk music, their short skirts

135

and gyrating hips leaving nothing to the imagination, much to the delight of the menfolk.

The party did not stop; as people left to visit other bars, more people would arrive to continue the happy atmosphere. Some women would even go home at 2.00am, only to return an hour later in a completely different outfit and continue to dance the night away.

At 5.00am I was exhausted, very tired, very sober, but very happy. I bid my friends a final 'Sretna Nova Godina' and returned to my apartment; there, from the veranda, I watched and listened to a town in the full throes of merriment. I could not come to terms with the intense feelings of happiness and contentment that welled up inside me, but I did sleep well.

Between New Year's Day and the Orthodox Christmas, the camp commander of SFOR appeared regularly on local television. Speaking through an interpreter, he announced the start of a new initiative called 'Operation Harvest'. This appeal was aimed directly at the citizens of Brčko District, and its objective was to get the local people to hand in weapons and explosives that had been kept after the war. In order to achieve this aim, a large tent had been erected on a grassed area in the middle of town and anyone could walk in and deposit their guns so that they could be destroyed.

The Orthodox New Year was soon to arrive, and the SFOR commander knew only too well how the midnight hour was going to be celebrated. Would the local people listen to his pleas and respond to the appeal by handing in their weapons?

Surprisingly, the answer was 'yes'!

Will and I met up for morning coffee as usual, but our conversation was interrupted by a local man entering the café bar. In his arms he carried a long anti-tank rocket launcher. He smiled at us, then placed the heavy weapon down onto the table and casually ordered a coffee. When he finished his drink, he lifted the weapon onto his shoulders and strolled off in the direction of the SFOR tent.

Moments later, an elderly woman shuffled her way passed with a string of six hand grenades draped around her shoulders like a French onion seller, and she too entered the green military tent.

Will and I could not contain ourselves; the scene was so surreal. It was simply the casual way that the local people went about their daily life. 'Let me see, I need eggs, butter, coffee, and a packet of digestive biscuits, and, oh yes, I must drop off six grenades and a thousand rounds of ammunition to SFOR!'

Tears of joy rolled down our cheeks; if only everyone could see this moment.

Each evening, the SFOR commander would invite the local TV station into the camp, to view the weapons that had been handed in. The stockpile was enormous; I had no idea that so many guns and explosive ordnance were still in the hands of the local community. Yes, it was accepted that most people had a pistol or a rifle, but here on television I could see things such as mines, grenades, bullets, mortar bombs and rockets, in addition to the many hundreds of pistols and high-powered rifles. Where did it all come from?

And, more to the point, how much more was there left?

I spent the Orthodox New Year at Stoja's home, as her family had invited me to spend the evening with them. I enjoyed a pleasant meal and drank far too much red wine, but then it was the New Year (again).

At midnight, we hugged and kissed to more shouts of *'Sretna Nova Godina!'*

Outside, we watched the beads of tracer fire in the starlight sky, followed by the occasional *boom* as a blast grenade exploded. It was clear to me that the local people still possessed a large quantity of guns and ammunition.

Operation Harvest would need to continue for a long while to come.

It was Newton who coined the phrase 'every action has an equal and opposite reaction', and in the case of Operation Harvest this proved to be very much the case.

When SFOR appealed to the local people to hand in weapons and explosives, the local children saw this as an opportunity to supplement their pocket money. The children thought that, in collecting unexploded ordnance and handing it over to UN personnel, they might receive a small cash reward. This had tragic consequences.

Matters came to a head when a group of children stood beside the road holding a live mortar bomb, waiting for someone in a UN truck to drive past. When an American IPTF officer did so, they tossed the bomb through the vehicle's open windows, where it landed on the passenger seat and bounced off into the footwell of the vehicle. The officer, in a natural state of blind panic, leapt from the vehicle, which continued on until it ended up in a ditch. Fortunately the shell did not explode, but the officer did need a few days off work to get over the ordeal.

Operation Harvest was temporarily suspended while a new programme was launched to stop the children from picking up these dangerous pieces of war.

Children, not having the experience of life to know danger, had devised a new way of disposing of land mines: now they would stand on the edge of a minefield and throw rocks into the long grass, applauding each time an anti-personnel mine exploded. The local police did well to quickly attend the many schools within the district to tell of the dangers of this practice.

I, too, assisted in this re-education of the children.

At the end of Nikola Pasic was a junior school; I had visited this school many times to talk to the teachers and children when I was working with the IPTF. Now, as a volunteer, I would demonstrate to the children the dangers by drawing a large circle in the playground; I placed an old tin can in the centre of this and invited the children to throw a rock to see if they could hit the can. Each time they missed they would have to take a step closer to the can, and by the time they could hit it they would be well and truly inside the circle.

I then explained that everyone inside the circle would be killed when the mine exploded and would therefore be out of the game.

This became a regular feature played by the children themselves during break times; I would rather have them doing that than doing it for real with deadly mines.

CHAPTER 11

GOOD TO BAD THEN EVEN WORSE

Christmas and New Year was well behind us, and what little snow had fallen quickly disappeared in the warm spring sunshine. Niko had now started his new job as a security officer at OHR, and this provided another excuse for a party.

We met up at the Galaxy. Niko took great delight in explaining his duties; it was plain to see that he enjoyed his new job, and I was very happy for him.

Yvette and Toma chose this occasion to announce their engagement. I had known Yvette since my first year in Brčko: a petite woman with a bubbly and infectious personality. She and Toma had kept their relationship a secret for months, but now she was keen to show the world her newfound love, as well as showing off the diamond ring that Toma had given to her.

The following morning I chose to stay in bed and write a letter to my daughter, but I was interrupted when the telephone rang; it was Dragan.

'Good morning, mate; you should switch on your TV and watch the news.'

As I had to wait for ten minutes for the news bulletin, I got up and showered. It was now that I noticed the small lump on the side of my neck, and this was tender when touched.

I quickly dismissed this, as the news was now starting on the television. The scene was shocking; divers were pulling lifeless bodies from a lake. I turned up the volume to find out what had occurred.

As the camera pulled back I quickly realised that the scene of the incident was the lake by Lončari, where Dragan, Niko and I had played a game of cricket on the floating pontoon that had been under construction. Now the pontoon was under water. The newsreader explained that the pontoon had been used to celebrate a wedding party, but the combined weight of 200 guests had caused the construction to collapse, spilling everyone into the lake and trapping many of them under the tarpaulin canopy. As the construction sank to the bottom, those people on the banks of the lake could hear the screams of panic as it dragged the guests under the water.

It was reported that at least ten of the party had drowned, including the bride and groom.

This was such a tragic end to what should have been a wonderful day of happy celebration.

After watching the news, I left the apartment and walked down to the port to share a cup of coffee with Stoja. As soon as I had said 'Good morning' she noticed the swelling on my neck and examined me more closely. The swelling had grown rapidly and caused me to flinch as Stoja ran her fingers over the lump.

'*Grem, ti treba doktor, brzo!*'

I assured her that I would see a doctor later that day, but she became more insistent. '*Ne polsi, ja hoce ti idem sad!*'

She was serious, and her demand that I should see a doctor straight away caused me to feel a little anxious, but I complied with her instructions and left.

My local language skills were OK but basic, and to talk to a doctor I needed a language assistant. I telephoned Dragan and arranged to meet at the Galaxy.

'Hello, mate; are you sick?'

'No, I feel fine, but I have this small lump on the side of my neck and Stoja insists that I see a doctor straight away.'

Dragan now examined my neck; a look of concern came across his face. 'Mate, I do not want to worry you, but this is not a small lump. I must agree with Stoja; you need to see a doctor straight away. Let us go now; I know of a good one.'

My main concern now was that I did not know what was wrong with me or how serious the condition was.

I climbed into Dragan's car and we drove to the doctor's private home. Dragan spoke for me and the doctor gestured for me to enter a small surgery. There I gave blood and urine samples with which he conducted a variety of tests, and then he spoke to Dragan.

'He asks are you allergic to penicillin?'

'No, not that I am aware of.'

'Good, then we must go to the hospital straight away.'

The doctor wrote out a prescription and handed it to Dragan; he then drove me to the hospital.

'So did he say what is wrong with me?'

'You have a serious infection from the local water and will need seven penicillin injections; the nurse will give you one each day.'

'Thank God for that; I was beginning to think I had cancer or something like that.'

'No, no, no, my grandfather had the same infection that you have, three days before he died!' He then left the room, smiling.

I was about to say something rude but was interrupted by the nurse, who invited me to drop my trousers and lie on the couch face down.

A doctor entered the room; he felt the lump on my neck and handed the nurse a small glass bottle from which she extracted the fluid contents with a syringe. She then wiped an area of my buttock with a medicated swab and gave me the injection, I was glad that it was painless.

Then she called Dragan back into the room and spoke to him.

'The nurse tells me that you must lie still for twenty minutes, and if you have any pain or start to feel bad then you must tell me so that the nurse can give you another injection to cancel the penicillin.'

'So I have to lie here with my bum in the air for twenty minutes; oh, what joy!'

There was a sudden flash of light, quickly followed by the auto-wind sound of a camera.

'Dragan, you sod!'

'You must lie still, mate; you do not want to have a bad reaction.' He then passed the camera to Beba, who was waiting outside the surgery door, giggling.

The nurse re-entered the room with a broad smile upon her face.

'So what has she found so amusing, then?' I asked Dragan.

'Oh, sorry, mate, I forgot to tell you, she said you could get dressed whenever you like!'

Dragan had had his moment of fun, but I was really grateful for his assistance; he really did put my mind at ease.

'Three days before he died, indeed!'

Dragan gave me a lift to Stoja's office down by the port, where I explained the problem to her and put her fears to rest. She was pleased that everything was going to be all right.

Every day for the next six days, Dragan picked me up from my apartment and drove me to the hospital to receive my daily injection. The course of treatment meant that I could not drink any alcohol, but the abstention was worth it

143

because by the fifth day the lump on my neck had completely disappeared and everything was back to normal.

It was during this week that a certain photograph appeared, pinned to the bar of the Galaxy; there in full glossy colour was my posterior being exposed to the world for all to see.

Mother's Day, or Mothering Sunday, finds its origins traced back to the religious celebration of the Holy Mother.

Back home in England we celebrate the day by telling Mum to stay in bed and enjoy receiving breakfast there. We also, on this day, send cards to speak words of affection and kindness, and do those homely chores that mothers do. Finally we cook the main meal of the day, and all of this to show our love and appreciation towards our mothers.

Brčko is no different, here the day is called 'Zena Dan' and it is celebrated during the first week of March. The menfolk take pride in cooking the main meal of the day, which is normally spit-roasted pig with an assortment of salad and bread.

On this day, Dragan was sitting in the living room, patiently waiting for me to finish shaving so that we could drive to Bijeljina to buy a full-length leather coat for my daughter, Lindsey.

Stepping out of the apartment, I could hear the unmistakable squealing of a pig, coming from the apartment opposite. Suddenly the door opened and out shot a small piglet followed by a young girl, whose outstretched arms ushered the piglet down the staircase.

'*Mrsc, mrsc, brzo, brzo*!' she said in a hushed voice.

'*Ne, ne, ne*!' came a shout, as out from the apartment dashed a harassed-looking man who stumbled down the staircase after the piglet, which was by now two floors below us and squealing loudly as it made a frantic bid for freedom.

144

Dragan and I both laughed and slowly made our way down to the ground floor. By the time we had stepped out onto the pavement, the piglet had reached a muddy area of ground, still being pursued by the now exhausted man.

All the noise and activity had now attracted an audience, as families from other apartments stood on their balconies to watch the hilarious scene that was unfolding below. The menfolk would shout words of encouragement to the man as he repeatedly dived towards the piglet in an effort to catch the elusive animal. The children, however, cheered each time the piglet leapt to one side to evade capture.

The chase continued for several minutes, then, in a last desperate lunge, the man caught hold of the piglet's hind leg and both rolled around in the mud as the man improved his grip on the squealing animal.

'Oopah!' came the cry from the audience of onlookers.

There he stood, covered from head to toe in black mud, the only discernible features of his face being his mouth and eyes. As a toast to his victorious effort, he raised an arm to acknowledge the applause from his neighbours.

'So why would a man keep a pig in a town centre apartment?'

Dragan laughed. 'Perhaps it is prettier than his wife, or maybe he intends to kill the pig in his apartment and then roast it on a barbecue.'

'Why kill it inside when he could do outside?'

'Because outside there is no water; inside he can kill it in the shower!'

'In the shower! That is disgusting; surely a butcher could have killed it for him?'

'No way, mate; he needs to save the blood and intestines so that he can make sausages. In Brčko we waste nothing!'

We chose to stop off at the bakery to have breakfast, and it was now that I realised that my wallet lay on the kitchen table in my apartment, so after breakfast we returned to collect it. As we drew to a halt outside the apartment block, there was my neighbour, standing over a roasting fire with the piglet turning on a spit.

'Well, at least he did not light his fire on the balcony.'

'Of course not; the intestines that hang on the washing line would get in the way!'

We both laughed out loud.

Following Mother's Day came Easter; it is a time of religious celebration. Unlike the West, Easter in Brčko had not become so commercialised that the original meaning had somehow become lost. The buying of chocolate eggs was a luxury that few could afford, so the boiling and hand painting of real eggs was the order of the day. These eggs would be given to friends and relatives as gifts and would be used by families to play a game during the evening.

Stoja had invited me to share 'Veliki Petak' or 'Good Friday' with her and her family, so, after I had attended church, I walked to her home. There I enjoyed a meal of fried fish, soup and a vegetable version of sarma, and, as usual, washed it all down with red wine.

Later, during the evening, we all sat in a circle on the floor. In the centre of the circle Stoja placed a bowl of beautifully decorated eggs; these had been dyed dark red in colour and then painted in a fine gold filigree pattern. We each took an egg. It seemed such a shame to me that these delicate Fabergé-style eggs were to be now destroyed to play a game, the object of which was to use the egg to tap the egg of the person next to you. If the eggshell broke, the egg had to be eaten and whoever had the unbroken egg was deemed the winner.

I was now into my third egg and began to question why Stoja's egg had not been broken by anyone. This suspicion had also crossed the minds of Milka and Rada, and both of them now wrestled with Stoja on the floor for possession of her egg, amid fits of giggled laughter.

Stoja relented and tossed her egg to me.

'You cheat, it is made of wood!'

'*Molim*?' she replied, trying to look innocent.

The wooden egg was placed upon the table and a fresh bowl of eggs was obtained from the kitchen, whereupon the game recommenced.

Again Stoja kept winning and was quickly set upon by her daughters. This devious woman had indeed secreted another false egg in the bowl and was now chased out of the house and around the garden by the two girls, only finding sanctuary by locking herself in the toilet!

I enjoyed this evening; it represented the perfect ideal of family life: no TV, no DVD and no computer games, just a simple bowl of eggs and a family sharing quality time.

The month of May was usually hot and sunny, so why was it raining? The confused weather conditions caused clouds of steam to rise off the hot road surface, creating a blanket of mist that rose no higher than one's waist and gave the early morning an eerie feel.

This morning, Will was very kindly giving me a lift to Sarajevo so that I could attend a meeting with the director of ICITAP, the international agency that I was hoping to join. I should have felt excited, but, for some strange reason, I had a sense of foreboding.

After entering the tall blue UN building, I made my way to the ICITAP office, where an Oriental woman who was the receptionist and director's secretary met me. She led me through to the director's office and introduced me a tall and politely-spoken man.

"Good morning, Graham; come in and take a seat. Sadly, I am the bearer of bad news"

He went on to explain that, due to a change of administration in America, all funding had been frozen pending a review of manpower, recruitment and budget requirements; this meant that my application was now put on hold. This was not the news I had hoped for, as now my time would be limited to the length of time my savings would last.

Will and I decided to drive to a Chinese restaurant in the town centre of Sarajevo. This served two purposes: allowing us to treat ourselves to a meal that could not be had in Brčko because there were no Chinese restaurants there, and giving us a place to sit and discuss a plan of action.

I decided that my best options were to find an alternative agency here in Bosnia or to return to England at the end of September to continue my degree studies and, when completed, apply to OHR or OSCE.

We finished our meal and returned to Brčko. I now needed to network; this was not a good day.

The next morning, I met up with the usual crowd for morning coffee at the café bar next to the local police station.

'Morning, Graham; how would you like to go and take a look at an old abandoned war train?'

'Yes, I would like that; I did not know that one existed!'

We boarded the vehicles and drove to a small village some twenty kilometres outside the district. The train was not hard to find, for, as we entered the village, a large notice stated, 'Here stands the war train that was abandoned by the Serbs who we defeated and forced out of our village.' I did not need to be told that 'we' meant the Bosnian Muslims who lived in the village.

The community leader of the village escorted our group to the train, and I was pleased that none of my friends, who were Serbian, made any ethnic comments, choosing instead to respect the fact that all sides had suffered many losses during the war.

The train turned out to be the rear two carriages, the coachwork having been removed, leaving just the chassis of the rolling stock. Onto this had been welded a solid steel fortress made of inch-thick plate metal with small portholes cut into the sides for guns to protrude.

Access to the inner sanctum of this metal monster was via a side door that also gave access to the adjoining carriage. From inside, I was better able to appreciate the full horror and noise that the soldiers onboard would have endured. The sun created beads of light through large holes; these had been created by anti-tank rockets which had torn their way into the structure, spreading shards of hot molten metal in all directions around the interior. The jagged pieces of metal all faced inwards and left the viewer in no doubt that this destruction had been caused by incoming shells and that, despite the thickness of the heavy metal shielding, conditions inside this machine of death would have been hell and life would be very short lived.

I ventured to the rear of the train; here I could see, mounted on the far end of the carriage, a Bofors anti-aircraft gun. This powerful weapon was very familiar to me, as I used to man such a weapon during my years with the Royal Air Force Regiment back in the 1970s. I also noted with a degree of surprise that the manufacture's plate showed this to have formally been a British gun.

Viewing the now twisted and splintered metal, I climbed into the ring of the number-four post, this had been the position I took when I operated the weapon. In my mind I replayed the roles of each man who would have assisted in the firing of this powerful gun.

'*Held, depress.*'

The safety catches applied and barrel lowered, so that I could rotate the handle that cocked the breach mechanism.

'*Elevate!*'

'*Set!*'

'*Held!*'

The number-three man loaded a clip of five enormous shells into the magazine.

'*Engage!*'

'*Auto set!*'

'*Fire!*'

And the gun would burst into loud explosions as each shell soared skywards.

When I used this weapon, the only thing I shot at was a target being towed by a plane. Now my mind tried to picture the men operating this piece of war machinery whilst under fire themselves.

Looking at the twisted and jagged panels that were meant to protect the gunners, I knew instinctively that life was measured in minutes, not days, weeks or years.

Death is not without pain.

CHAPTER 12

SUMMER CELEBRATION

Mosquitoes buzzed around my head with that annoying 'zing' sound as I walked along the pavement, but I paid no attention to these as my mind was full of questions and future hopes.

I had just spent the afternoon at Stoja's sister's home, as she was celebrating a saint day and had very kindly thought to invite me. It had been a large gathering, comprising aunts, uncles, parents and grandparents, not to mention the children, but it was a very pleasant way to spend the day.

Now, however, amid the mosquitoes, I had arrived at the Galaxy and chose to sit with Toma and Yvette.

Shortly afterwards, Niko entered; he looked happy and excited. '*Cao kume!*'

'*Cao Niko, sat radis, sta bilo novo?*'

'Today me and my family return to our village of Vitanovic; our home has been rebuilt!'

'That is great news; do you need help to move the furniture?'

'That would be great, and then we could have a barbecue outside.'

Until now, Niko and his family had temporarily occupied a house belonging to another Serbian family, but they would soon return to reclaim their home. As a show of respect and kindness, Niko's mother and sister cleaned the house from top to bottom, while the rest of us loaded furniture into a van and transported this to their new home.

The house did look smart, but the donor aid would only provide a living area on the ground floor. The rooms upstairs were left unfinished and needed doors, windows and plaster work on the bare brick walls. There was no urgency to do this, as Niko could comfortably live downstairs until he was able to complete the work.

My mind compared the present house with the pile of bricks and rubble that I had seen just a few months earlier; it was indeed a big transformation.

I was very happy for Niko and his family; it was good to see the village of Vitanovici Gornji getting back to its pre-war harmony. If I had any wishes for the village, then it would be to see the rebuilding of the Orthodox church that now lay as a burnt-out, destroyed building.

Niko's father had killed a pig, and this now roasted on a spit over an open fire; the women, meanwhile, were busy preparing a salad. The rest of us menfolk did what all men do at barbecues: stand about talking and drinking beer; this scene could have been repeated anywhere in the world.

Then, as we sat, Niko's Croat neighbours arrived, bringing bread, wine and Rakija, making them most welcome. They joined us by the fire, and Niko introduced me to his guests.

As I watched the interaction between the two ethnic families, I was forced to wonder why there had been a war in the first place, for here beside an open fire people talked like long lost friends, and it was now that I was to learn an amazing fact.

Niko and his Croatian friend had more or less grown up together in the same village. Both Croatia and Yugoslavia required men between the ages of 18 and 21 to do one year of national service in the army, and as a result both were despatched to their respective countries to do this. Then war broke out and both found themselves sitting on the banks of the River Sava, Niko on the Bosnian side, his friend on the Croatian side, and during the day each would blissfully shoot at the other, totally unaware of each other's position along the river bank. Yet, during the night, each would write letters, even sending cigarettes and food parcels to each other.

'I would have been full of sadness if I had shot him by accident!' said Niko.

For them, the war was a distant memory that was best forgotten and not mentioned.

The fire burned late into the evening and mosquitoes were buzzing all around, the female of the species being particularly annoying, as it was these that drilled into the skin to gorge on my blood.

Niko showed me the new pigs and chickens that he had recently purchased; these would ensure a continuous supply of food for the family for many coming years.

The land to the rear of Niko's house stretched far into the distance and was planted with sweetcorn; this was to be dried and given to the pigs and chickens as feed. The fact that no chemicals were used on the crops and no animals were force-fed in battery houses meant that all the food they produced was natural, nourishing and healthy; now that is what I call eco-farming.

It was around 10.30pm when we retired to the house; more food was prepared and bottles of beer passed to all.
Niko switched on the television and flicked through the channels to see what was on; he stopped to view the scenes of an angry riot. '*Beograd*!' he exclaimed.

Belgrade was going through turbulent times. Milošević, in a bid to re-establish his authority, had called an election, and the polls were showing that he was losing the vote. When the ballot results were counted, Milošević won, but there was a strong suspicion that votes had been tampered with and protests were breaking out all over the city.

Then the opposition party took an unprecedented gamble and, under the cover of darkness, broke into the polling station's headquarters and copied all the ballot results. The case was proven beyond all doubt; Milošević had forced the auditors to transfer votes from the opposition party and add them to the Milošević camp, and the opposition party wasted no time in finding a sympathetic TV station to publicise the evidence.

The people of Belgrade were outraged; rioting broke out all over the city. Tension within the country rose to a dangerous high when a Milošević supporter shot dead a supporter of the opposition party. There was now a real danger of civil war within Serbia.

A serious look of concern came across the face of Niko. 'You must stay here tonight, my friend; there will be crazy people about the town tonight.'

I accepted the offer, common sense being the better part of valour. We spent the night glued to the TV set, watching each bulletin to see if things were getting out of hand in Belgrade.

In the morning, Niko drove me back to Brčko; there I met up with Will.

'Morning, Will; did you see the news last night?'

'Sure did; some local idiot blew up a UN pickup with a hand grenade while it was parked outside a monitor's accommodation, and three pickups were stolen as well.'

Niko was right; there were crazy people about the town.

'SFOR have raised the alert level and are preparing the U.S base in case we need to evacuate from the town!'

This was not an overreaction by the international agencies; we were all well aware that, if civil war did erupt within Serbia, the repercussions would quickly reverberate through to Brčko; we were, after all, only 150 kilometres down the road.

Dragan was already wise to this and, as a caring friend to this Englishman, had arranged an escape route through

Croatia to Zagreb; from there I could catch a flight back to England.

This effort was not to cause concern, but it was always better to be prepared for the unexpected; if civil war was to occur then Brčko was not the place for an international to be.

The tension continued for the following week, and during this time I chose to stay in my apartment or stay at Stoja's house, as she would arrange for me to be collected by car. It would have been naive in the extreme to assume that, just because I had many friends within the town, I did not have enemies as well. The international staff followed the same example and were instructed to remain in their accommodation; spending time in café bars during the evening was definitely not a good idea. Everyone watched the news on TV, intently listening to each bulletin in case something new had occurred.

The strange thing was that nobody that I knew supported Milošević; all seem to want him voted out of office, and, judging by the reports that were now coming from Belgrade, this looked like a real possibility. The people of the town knew that if Milošević lost his political protection he would be handed over to the UN to face the war crimes trials at The Hague. Few seemed to object to this idea, although most thought he would escape capture by fleeing to Russia or South America.

The capture of the man who led the army, Radovan Karadžić, was a different story; he seemed to have more supporters, and it was not long before the lyrics of an old Serbian folk song were amended to read '*Dok se zemlja oko sunca krece, Radovana uhvatiti nece*': 'while the Earth moves around the sun, Radovan will never be found'.

Tonight, while enjoying a meal with Stoja and her family, our conversation was interrupted by a news bulletin on TV: Milošević had announced his resignation from office and had been placed under house arrest.

At first there was silent disbelief, as it was well known that the state-run TV companies were prone to bending the truth. But now onto the screen came the US ambassador, and he too confirmed the reports that were coming from Belgrade.

The people of Brčko were jubilant and drove about the town, honking car horns and waving Serbian tri-coloured flags from the open windows of their vehicles; others fired pistols into the air. The fears of anti-UN riots were quickly washed away, as the local people celebrated the appointment of a new leader to the former Yugoslavia.

I knew that the town would party tonight, and party they certainly did! Guns were fired well into the night, café bars played loud music and people continued to drive around, waving flags and blowing whistles.

It appeared to me that the people were not solely celebrating the end of Milošević but preferred instead to celebrate a more democratic beginning. Having spent the past six years in poverty and depression, the people of Brčko gained a renewed sense of hope for the future.

The new president of Yugoslavia was a liberal nationalist and recognised the fact that, if his country's infrastructure and economy was to grow and prosper, he would have to work with the United Nations. This new and open dialogue with political leaders of western countries, coupled with a more willing acceptance of the mandates laid down by the UN regarding human rights violations, ensured that Serbia received donor aid in the form of project funding and specialist advisors for a variety of government agencies.

Sadly, not everyone shared the same vision, and in less than two years the new president of Yugoslavia was assassinated by Mafia members who supported the Milošević camp.

If the local people were not celebrating a saint day, the next best excuse for a party was a wedding; in Brčko, a person got married on a Saturday, and today was Saturday. Dragan was to have the honour of being best man to Milan, a local Serb, who was a skilled car mechanic and had started up his own business from the garage of his uncle's home. Milan had very kindly invited me as a guest of the groom's family, and for me this was a wonderful opportunity as it meant that I could witness first-hand the entire wedding day customs, a ceremony that few western eyes were ever privileged to see.

The day started early, around 8.00am, and, although I was still in bed, Dragan's constant banging on the door ensured that I was not going stay asleep. Having forced myself to get out of bed and into the shower, I dressed and walked downstairs to find Dragan was waiting in his car.

'Good morning, mate; did I wake you? Our wedding parties start at 6.00am, so you are two hours late already!'

'Who in their right mind would get married at six in the bloody morning? By the way, good morning, Dragan!'

My body was slow to respond first thing in the morning, but after a short while I gathered my senses and was human again.

Approaching the driveway of Milan's home, I was met by his uncle, who held in his hands a tray of small glasses that were filled with Rakija. These were being offered as a blessing to the family's home that I was about to enter, so I took one and downed the drink in one go.

The fiery spirit hit the pit of my empty stomach and exploded with the ferocity of a thermonuclear device, sending a hot flush rising through the chest that caused the throat to contract and made me cough.

In short, it definitely woke me up!

'*Cao Nikola, dobro utro i dobro dosli.*'

'*Hvala vama Milane, dobro utro.*'

Milan invited me to sit next to him at the long wooden table under the white gazebo that stood in the rear garden.

Dragan meanwhile, tended to his duties, which at this moment meant receiving the other male guests and offering the small glasses of Rakija.

It was explained to me that, while the guys were coming to Milan's home, his bride-to-be was doing exactly the same, receiving all of the female guests. This period of the ceremony was called the 'wedding breakfast', and for the meal we ate fish soup, fried fish and bread, all washed down with a bottle of beer.

Breakfast continued until around midday and, judging by the large quantity of alcohol on display, I got the feeling that it would be wise to drink very slowly. Overindulgence at this hour of the day would probably cause me to pass out in an alcoholic haze and miss out on the rest of the day's events; it was, after all, only 8.30am.

By mid-morning the tent was crowded and everyone was drinking and laughing. Niko arrived and I felt more relaxed having a familiar face to talk to; his arrival had been delayed because he had to work the night shift.

While we were talking a little girl tugged at my jacket, wanting me to kneel down, so I did. She then pinned a small white flower to the lapel of my jacket, and in return, as tradition demanded, I placed a small offering of cash into the girls flower basket.

The outside of Milan's home was now more representative of a German national car park, as most if not all of the vehicles around the property were of German origin. We now *en masse* climbed into these to conduct the first of the town centre parades.

I had seen wedding convoys driving through the town many times, but this was the first time I had taken part, and it quickly became a hilarious farce. The convoy of vehicles caused chaos at every traffic junction and the constant honking of car horns deafened the people standing on the roadside. I was travelling with Niko and, due to excessive use of the horn, the device overheated and now made rude flatulent noises instead of a tuneful beep.

From the town, we drove to the home of the bride-to-be, and upon arrival we again went through the tradition of blessing the house with the drinking of more Rakija. All of the men went to the long marquee that stood in the garden, where more soup, bread and beer was consumed.

The bride, however, was nowhere to be seen, as tradition demands that she be locked in the home of her mother and the best man, Dragan in this case, must gain her freedom by offering money to the girl's mother, who waits inside the house beside the door.

This was a wonderful custom, so all of the guests gathered to watch the bidding take place.

Dragan approached the door and knocked; the door opened and he offered 250 marks to the girl's mother. She declined the offer and slammed the door shut.

He knocked again and presented 400 marks; again the mother refused the offer with a slam of the door in his face.

He tried a third time and pleaded with the woman to accept an offer of 500 marks, and again the door slammed shut.

The crowd now encouraged Dragan to increase the offer to a much larger amount, and so he knocked at the door and offered 700 marks; at this the woman took the money and Dragan rushed inside to rescue the bride-to-be.

Both now appeared in the doorway, the bride dressed in a very ornately decorated white wedding gown and looking resplendent. Dragan dutifully gave her hand to Milan, who was patiently waiting outside.

'OOPAH!' the crowd cheered, and, as the music band played traditional lively folk songs, we all made our way back to the marquee to eat the wedding lunch and drink a toast to the bride and groom's future happiness and good fortune.

During the meal, the little girl from before approached me; she pinned another white flower onto the other lapel of my jacket and, as before, I placed a small offering of cash into her basket.

We all now returned to our cars and drove to the council offices to witness the signing of the register; from there, we travelled to the church for the wedding ceremony.

Inside the church, candles refracted the light from the large and ornate chandeliers that hung from the ceiling, casting a soft light on the beautifully painted icons of the different saints. Everybody remained standing. The bride and groom were beside the altar, facing the priest; the best man and the best lady stood behind the bride and groom; all four were holding lit candles.

Then the priest read a prayer and placed fine golden crowns, encrusted with precious stones, onto the heads of the bride and groom. He gave the couple a blessing and then swapped over the crowns. All four walked in a circle as the priest led the congregation in prayer.

The service concluded and the party began, starting with another convoy of cars that drove through the town, honking their car horns.

We wound our way to the hotel, where a reception was held; more eating, drinking and dancing was had, ably assisted by a live folk music band.

At midnight, traditionally, a large silver tray is carried around the room and on this you place a gift of cash. There is no fixed amount; you give whatever you wish to give, or, more to the point, what you can afford. 20 marks (£8.00) seemed to be the average. The money collected was counted up and used to pay for the reception party, and whatever was left over was given to the bride and groom to spend on a honeymoon.

This was how to get married Balkan style, and what a most wonderful day it was.

CHAPTER 13

JUST ANOTHER DAY

I had now lived in Brčko for a long while, and during this time I had witnessed things that had shocked me, surprised me and endeared the town and its people to me.

Family and family life were a very important facet of the way of life of the Bosnian people, and since moving into my flat I came to meet all of my neighbours, one of whom was a single mother who had a five-year-old daughter. Each and every day, the little girl would ride her pink toddler-sized bicycle up and down the street, and, although she always played alone, I knew her mother was never far away.

This was not a neglected child; she was dearly loved and cared for, but, more importantly, she was safe, and I began to wonder why. The answer was simple, for while she played alone she was under the protective gaze of all the residents in the street.

I found myself comparing this 'shared nursery supervision' with life for a child back in England and came to the conclusion that, while we would like to think that our children are safe, the truth is that danger lurks on every corner. Often in England one would hear mothers calling their young ones to come inside the safety of the home, this protective nature being both normal and natural. But here in Brčko, this fear did not seem to exist; although the girl was well versed in not talking to strangers, she was encouraged to speak to relatives and neighbours, and I was a neighbour.

Today was the little girl's birthday, and as a gift her mother had given her a budgerigar; the budgie would sit in its cage outside on the veranda and chirp constantly.

As usual, I walked down the street towards my apartment; the girl rode around me in circles on her bicycle.

'*Dobro dan Nikola.*'

'*Dobro dan, kako si danas?*'

'*Super, danas moj rodjendan.*'

'*Sretan rodjendan.*'

The child's mother then came out onto the veranda and began to hang freshly washed clothes on the washing line.

'*Cao Nikola.*'

I bade her good day and asked if she would object to my giving a small gift to her daughter. She told me that it was OK and thanked me for asking, so, with that, I walked off to a nearby toyshop.

I cast my eyes along the shelf of cuddly toys and came across a small black gorilla that had an amusing feature. When I clapped my hands, the gorilla would nod his head and sing a Turkish song called 'Kiss Kiss'; this would later be a chart hit in the UK.

I chose the toy and told the shop assistant that it was a gift for a little girl; she carefully wrapped it in suitable gift paper and tied a pink ribbon around it.

I now returned to my street and saw the girl sitting on the tiled steps; her mother stood on the veranda of her ground floor apartment. I handed the gift to the child and said, '*Sretan rodjendan.*'

She took the present from my hand but then hesitated and looked at her mother.

'*Ne problem,*' said her mother in approval.

The child's face beamed with excitement as she tore open the paper wrapping, and then, on looking at the gorilla, she gave a confused frown.

Clapping my hands together caused the gorilla to burst into song, and it nodded its head in time with the tune of

'Kiss Kiss'. Fits of giggles erupted from the girl as she proceeded to stop and start the gorilla by repeated clapping.

'*Hvala lijepo Nikola*,' said the child's mother.

'*Hvala vama*,' I replied, and walked off towards my apartment.

I had only taken a few steps when I heard the girl call my name; I turned around and instinctively knelt down as she ran towards me. She threw her arms around my neck and kissed me on the cheek.

'*Hvala puno*,' she said.

But she did not have to thank me; her beaming smile was thanks enough.

I continued up the stairs to my apartment and wondered just how long it would take for the child's mother to grow to dislike the constant singing of 'Kiss Kiss'.

The summer wore on. It was an unbearably hot and sticky night, and I found myself lying on my sofa bed, staring up at the ceiling.

Suddenly the room lit up with a bright green flash of light, quickly followed by an almighty crash that shook the building. Pictures that hung on the wall fell to the floor and plates that sat on the shelf in the kitchen now lay smashed in the sink.

I quickly ran out onto the balcony to see what had happened; other residents of the apartment block were doing the same.

'*Cao Nikola, sta radis?*'

'*Ja ne znam.*'

I could not offer an explanation to my neighbour as to what had occurred, but soon flames could be seen coming from the roof of a bungalow on the other side of the street. Down below, people were running across the road towards the bungalow, so I quickly threw on some clothes and went downstairs to see what assistance I could give.

Two lines of people now formed a chain, one line passing buckets of water to douse the fire, the other passing back pieces of furniture, which were stacked along the pavement. Upon a chair sat the elderly resident of the property.

I slotted into the line of water carriers and passed a bucket from one man to another, during which I asked if a bomb had caused the explosion.

'*Ne veliki bomba, veliki munja*!' replied the man next to me, pointing to the clouds above.

So lightning was the cause of all this commotion, and, as if on cue, another flash and rumble of thunder followed.

It was not long after that the fire truck arrived; we stood back and watched as the fireman quickly dealt with the flames.

The women now joined their husbands, carrying bottles of Rakija and small glasses; these were passed to all including myself, and after downing a glass of the fiery spirit I returned to my apartment for a well-deserved shower and a welcome sleep.

When morning arrived, Niko was ringing my doorbell.

'*Did you see, how you say, flashing last night*?' he asked excitedly.

My mind instantly pictured a man in a raincoat, exposing himself, and this caused me to smile. 'I think you mean lightning; that is our word for '*munja*'; yes, it struck the house across the street and started a fire.'

Niko stepped out onto the balcony while I boiled water for a coffee. 'Did anyone get hurt?'

'No, just a few burnt timbers.'

I passed Niko a mug of coffee and offered him a cigarette. He then told me about a new tractor that the residents of his village had clubbed together and purchased; it was second hand but reliable and would take care of all the ploughing. To the residents of Vitanovici this was an important asset if next year's crop of corn was to be planted to provide feed for the animals, which in turn fed everybody.

Outside, the weather was behaving rather strangely: one day would be unbearably hot, the next it would rain heavily, and this morning it rained as Niko gave me a lift into town.

The town's drainage system could not cope with sudden downpours and it was not long before some of the roads became flooded. One such area was the road to Stoja's house where it passed under the railway bridge. In order to keep the track level, the road dipped, but the pavements continued along at the same height and passed under the bridge with just enough room for a person to walk under.

The locals were used to this area flooding and simply chose to drive along the pavements in their cars. The American SFOR were not so well informed, however, and decided that US advanced technology meant that a trivial thing such as a flooded road would not and could not stop a fully armoured, all-terrain, Humvee 4x4 patrol vehicle.

On the other hand...

I could only imagine the embarrassment that the soldiers must have felt as they sat on top of their large black and green vehicles, which were now buried up to their windshields in water, waiting for the recovery truck to pull them out. The local people wasted no time in teasing them with offers of a lift in the battered ten-year-old Yugoslav cars that seemed to be indestructible in Brčko. To add insult to injury, the local fire service came and sucked up all the water, thus removing any evidence to support the soldiers' claim of running into deep water.

It was simple incidents like this that brought humour to the town, and, for the local people, humour was desperately needed. Fortunately, even SFOR soldiers have a good sense humour and were happy to laugh at their own misfortune, bless them.

An entrepreneurial boat builder had hit on the idea of converting an old steel river barge into a Mississippi-style riverboat; this was to be used as a restaurant and music bar, with a casino being installed in the belly of the craft. When the work had been completed, the craft did look the part, although I was pleased to see that it was permanently anchored to the banks of the River Sava.

Will, Dragan and I chose the riverboat as a pleasant way of spending a lazy afternoon; the warmth of the sun ably assisted by a soft gentle breeze made it preferable to sit outside on the open deck at the stern of the craft.

With a bottle of beer in hand I viewed the calm and picturesque scene that lay before me. Water gurgled as the current moved it along under the steel bridge that spanned the two tree-lined embankments. The linear effect of these caused the river to fade into a dot in the far distance as it made its way towards Belgrade, where it would join forces with the mighty Danube.

There was no need for conversation, such was the peace and quiet; I simply closed my eyes and tilted back my head to allow my throat and chest to better absorb the sunrays.

BOOM! came the explosion, the shock wave hitting my body with a thud.

Will and I instinctively ducked down, but Dragan remained on his bar stool, totally unshaken, and continued to drink from his bottle of beer. 'Did I miss something?'

'What the bloody hell was that?' asked Will

'The Croats are mine clearing along the bank of the river!' replied Dragan as we retook our seats and watched the plume of smoke mushroom up into the sky.

The river at this point was about 300 metres wide, so we all sat and watched in fascination as the Croatian army set the charges to blow up another group of mines.

BOOM, and a host of trees that lined the riverbank fell over into the river and floated off downstream.

It seemed strange to be sitting in the sunshine, drinking beer and enjoying a meal to the sound of controlled explosions just a few hundred metres away. Back home, the entire town would have been evacuated; such is our protective nature and the love of dramatics by those in authority.

But the de-mining was becoming a nuisance, so we decided to leave and return to the centre of town.

Niko now joined us as we sat outside the Fontana café bar, which, as the name suggests, had a fountain. The fountain was in the form of a boy and a girl holding onto the tail of a fish, but, sadly, it was in dire need of servicing. Rather than a spray of water being emitted from the fins, a thin trickle ran down the front of the fish, and this had now turned to green mould.

'Did you hear the bangs?' asked Niko.

'Yes; we were watching, but it is better to sit here.'

'They should clear mines the Serbian way.'

'And how is that, Niko?'

'We herd sheep through the long grass: no bangs means no mines; lots of bangs still mean no mines but you do have lots of popcorn!'

I had to think for a second as my mind worked out the connection between sheep and popcorn, then I smiled. 'You are such a plonker, Niko.'

'*Molim?*' he replied rhetorically.

A few metres away, children drove around in circles in battery-powered jeeps that could be hired for just a few marks. The children were quite safe, as the area had been cordoned off for the event, although I feared for the safety of the parents who were supervising them.

I noted that one of the children, a boy, was a particularly aggressive driver and would collide into the other vehicles on purpose. One such vehicle was being driven by a girl of about seven who was proudly showing her parents her driving skills. After the boy had bashed into the rear of the girl's jeep, she pulled away and drove in a complete circle, then, as she passed the boy, she waved a fist and raised the middle finger at him. This shocked the boy so much that he drove into the leg of his father, who promptly yanked him out of jeep by his ear.

The girl laughed as she weaved from side to side in celebration; we too laughed and had to accept that girl power had come to Brčko.

Niko then told us of a news item that he had seen earlier during the day. It appeared that, as a result of the war, nobody bothered to pay their electricity bill. This left the state-run electric company with no funds with which to pay the employees' wages. The head of the electric company appealed to the citizens of the Republic of Srpska, saying that if everyone paid 50 marks the remaining debt would be written off. This offer had obvious merits and so the people paid.

The head of the company, now being in possession of a couple of million marks, suddenly decided that life in South America was a far better option to life in Bosnia and promptly left the country, taking the money with him.

'No surprises there, then; I just hope everyone paid with counterfeit money!' said Dragan.

Will returned from his office and sat down. 'Graham, I have just had a call from the community leader of Boderista asking we could assist in resolving a problem; would you be able to come along to the meeting?'

'Certainly; did he say what the problem was?

'Something about the bridge needing to be repaired, but we will know more tomorrow.'

The small town of Boderista sat on the edge of Brčko District; it was a predominately Muslim town before the war and remains as such today. Will, Dragan, Beba and I sat in a café bar in the centre of town, and after a short wait we were joined by the community leader and two local police officers.

The problem was simple; to gain access to the town, a vehicle would have to cross a small wooden bridge. The bridge was in urgent need of repair and the local community did not have the funds to do this, so we were being asked if we could assist.

Now, by a strange quirk of luck, the bridge over the Sava River had just been strengthened and refurbished by British and American engineers. As a result of the completed work, a large number of 'railway sleeper'-type wooden beams had been left unused and simply stood on the riverbank.

We returned to Brčko, where Will drove to the American base to speak to the US camp commander and seek permission to donate the leftover beams to the community of Boderista. When he returned he looked pleased.

'So how did the meeting go?'

'Great; not only will he donate the wood, but he is willing to arrange for his engineers to assist in the rebuilding of the bridge.'

This was good news, and, from SFOR's point of view, it would be good PR for the US military.

Will however, was looking for an angle from which the local police could be actively involved and share in some of the credit, as this would assist in cementing the relationship between the police and local community. He had the idea of getting the officers to assist in the dismantling of the old bridge alongside members of the community and, to ensure maximum effect, made a call to the local TV station to invite them to film the work being done.

The completed project was a credit to everyone involved and in a strange way was very symbolic, but, then again, it was just another day in Brčko.

CHAPTER 14

TIME TO RING THE CHANGE

No matter how hard we try to promote peace and harmony throughout the world, it seems that someone somewhere is determined to cause a problem. The pressures and demands put upon the United Nations increase daily, and this creates a shortage of manpower and funding to ensure stability and peace.

After Bosnia came Kosovo and then the continued problems in the Gulf States. There are about a hundred different places at any one time that have a need for UN peacekeepers in one form or another; the sky blue beret is a familiar sight throughout the world and is an accepted sign of neutrality.

Sadly, as one country increases its manpower, another suffers by a reduction of the same; Brčko and the rest of Bosnia were no different.

It should be remembered that the war had ended only six years ago, and if one were to compare the advances achieved by the Bosnian people, aided by the UN, with, say, the reintegration of Berlin after the Second World War, one might find it easier to understand just what it is that the UN can achieve.

So, as more authority is handed over to local agencies and government bodies, Bosnia continues to move forward in leaps and bounds, but the work is far from over and much more needs to be done to ensure to continued growth of the country's infrastructure and stability.

As the requirement for monitors is reduced, so is the need for language assistants, and many found themselves being made redundant or transferred to work in other parts of the country.

Branka left the UN to give birth to her child and concentrated more on the running of her dental practice; her husband had now returned from Belgrade and, having qualified as a doctor, set up a surgery in a room next door to Branka's.

Sinisa resigned from the UN as a language assistant and continues to run his '*teretana*' or gym.

Srecko and his wife Sandra moved to Sarajevo and continue to work for the UN as language assistants.

Beba left the UN and moved to Spain, and there she got married.

Zjelko now works in the town of Bihać as a language assistant.

Damir now lives with his wife in Novi Sad but continues to work as a language assistant in Bijeljina.

Sladjana continues to work as a cashier at a bank in Brčko town centre.

Milan got a job servicing air-conditioning systems at the American air base.

Neso found a job delivering medical supplies to all parts of Bosnia.

Dragan was sent to Bihać with Zjelko, but he has since secured a language assistant's post in the town of Orase, which is closer to Brčko and his new bride Danka, who runs a wedding dress shop.

Niko continues to proudly work as a security officer at OHR.

Will is still working in Brčko.

Rada, who is always feeling fine, is studying for her degree.

Milka, having achieved her degree, now works for Mercy Corps, advising families on micro-credit programs.

Stoja continues to work as a cashier for a local bank down by the port.

Sinisa Kisic is still the Mayor of Brčko.

Pero Duric continues to be a police chief.

And so life goes on for the people of Brčko District. I too must now move on.

To round off my stay in Brčko, I invited my daughter Lindsey to visit the town for a holiday; as usual she was treated like a princess by the local people, who made her most welcome and showered her gifts.

Lindsey and I looked out of the rear window of Niko's car as we crossed the steel bridge that spanned the River Sava.

'Bye bye, Brčko; thank you for a wonderful time,' she said as she waved at the Bosnian border police, who were now getting smaller as Niko drove us away, heading for Zagreb airport.

Her words were so true.

I hated goodbyes, so I avoided the issue, and when Niko dropped us off at the airport it was a simple shake of the hand that did the speaking.

'Vidimose kume.'

THE END